SIR HALLEY STEWART TRUST: PUBLICATIONS

Volume 8

DELINQUENCY AND CHILD NEGLECT

DELINQUENCY AND CHILD NEGLECT

HARRIETT WILSON

Routledge
Taylor & Francis Group

LONDON AND NEW YORK

First published in 1962 by George Allen & Unwin Ltd.

This edition first published in 2025
by Routledge
4 Park Square, Milton Park, Abingdon, Oxon OX14 4RN

and by Routledge
605 Third Avenue, New York, NY 10158

Routledge is an imprint of the Taylor & Francis Group, an informa business

British Library Cataloguing in Publication Data
A catalogue record for this book is available from the British Library

ISBN: 978-1-032-88962-7 (Set)
ISBN: 978-1-032-80488-0 (Volume 8) (hbk)
ISBN: 978-1-032-80581-8 (Volume 8) (pbk)
ISBN: 978-1-003-49750-9 (Volume 8) (ebk)

DOI: 10.4324/9781003497509

Publisher's Note
The publisher has gone to great lengths to ensure the quality of this reprint but points out that some imperfections in the original copies may be apparent.

Disclaimer
The publisher has made every effort to trace copyright holders and would welcome correspondence from those they have been unable to trace.

This book is a re-issue originally published in 1962. The language used and views portrayed are a reflection of its era and no offence is meant by the Publishers to any reader by this re-publication.

Delinquency
and
Child Neglect

HARRIETT WILSON

Published for
THE SIR HALLEY STEWART TRUST

GEORGE ALLEN & UNWIN LTD
RUSKIN HOUSE
MUSEUM STREET LONDON

Printed in Great Britain
in 11 *point Juliana type*
BY EAST MIDLAND PRINTING CO. LTD.
BURY ST. EDMUNDS

To Morris Ginsberg

PREFACE

The present investigation arose out of a request made by the local Juvenile Delinquency Committee to the University for research concerning the causation of delinquency in certain areas of the city, where there is a relatively high incidence of juvenile crime. As these areas are the main living quarters of the poorer section of the population and of families who had come to the notice of the local authority because of suspected child neglect, it was decided to broaden the field of study into an investigation concerning the relationship between such families and juvenile delinquency. Since many families willingly co-operated in making details of their lives available, the city shall be known as 'Seaport'.

I am greatly indebted to the numerous statutory and voluntary bodies who allowed statistical use to be made of their records, and in particular to the Medical Officer of Health and the Chief Constable. I should like to express my gratitude to all those who so generously gave me of their time and assisted this enquiry in many ways.

CONTENTS

PREFACE 9

I Trends in juvenile-delinquency studies 13

II Aims and methods of the Seaport survey 23

III The parents 40

IV The children 64

V Housing conditions 81

VI Performance inadequacy 96

VII Juvenile delinquency: the facts 112

VIII Juvenile delinquency: an interpretation 123

IX Conclusions 146

X Some practical proposals 160

APPENDICES 165

BIBLIOGRAPHY 189

INDEX 193

CHAPTER I

TRENDS IN JUVENILE DELINQUENCY STUDIES

'THE study of the criminal phenomenon,' says a recent Unesco Report, 'must be taken up in a new perspective, from the point of view of man and his needs, and not from that of repression and its techniques.' We have, indeed, come a long way since the days of Lombroso, when the concept of criminal propensity was seriously discussed. The psychiatric literature of today stresses the point that criminality is not a specific mental aberration, but that it must be seen as a symptom only which may arise in conjunction with a variety of underlying problems. Defect of mind, organic diseases, psycho-neuroses, or psychoses may produce delinquent behaviour; and similarly the environment may bring about the formation of anti-social character traits.

While the psychiatric literature views the problem of crime from the individual angle of motivation, the sociological literature has been mainly concerned with environmental conditions, and interest has centred predominantly on underprivileged areas. Burt (1925), in the first large-scale enquiry that made use of a control group, showed that over one-half of London's juvenile delinquents came from poor or very poor homes, which formed only thirty per cent of the general population at that time. The *New Survey of London Life and Labour* which was compiled a few years later gives the numbers of arrests made per 10,000 of population of different economic grades, and shows that unskilled workers and others actually living below the poverty line produced 28 criminals per 10,000 population, whereas skilled workers and the middle classes produced less than nine criminals per 10,000 population. Bagot (1941) in his Liverpool study found that eighty-five per cent of delinquents lived below standards that were considered necessary for the 'bare essentials of a civilized life'. Mannheim (1948) found in Cambridge that delinquents came mainly from the poorer strata of the community, and Ferguson (1952) showed that in Glasgow delinquency was concentrated in slum areas. Wootton (1959) examines twenty-one criminological investigations and comes to the conclusion that most of the criminals come from the lower social classes. The surveys on which her findings are based were carried out in Great Britain, the United States and in Sweden. It would indeed seem that the ancient rhyme which lumps the thief with poor man and beggarman has been sociologically proved to be correct.

How are we to understand this correlation between poverty and criminality? That there is no direct relationship is obvious, since we know that not all poor people are criminals even though many criminals are poor. In trying to find an answer let us first turn to American literature, which has been leading for many years in aetiological interpretation. We find there such concepts as that of the culture conflict, or the ecological concept of slum-area delinquency, or that of normlessness or *anomie*, or that of the working-class boy's frustration solution. Can any of these explanations help us to understand why certain people in Britain turn into criminals and others do not? The idea of a culture conflict has been elaborated by MacIver (1937), who examined the problems of large-scale immigration into the United States. He speaks about 'a difficult transitional stage . . . in which the younger generation, finding the ways of their parents despised in the larger community into which their schooling, their work, and their play initiate them, revolt from the family traditions and reject the nearer social controls before they have acquired the discipline of experience. Such a state of disorganization is at least suggested by the prevalence of delinquency among these groups. An undue eagerness to "americanize" the children of immigrants may exaggerate the problem.' Here we are already faced with problems peculiar to the United States; a country of which only three-fifths of the population today is of British and Irish origin. Benians (1946) reminds us that we do well to remember when talking to an American that, while he may be descended from a Pilgrim Father, it is more likely that he is the son of a Bavarian peasant or a Scandinavian farmer or an Italian shopkeeper or a Greek shepherd or a Polish mechanic. This ethnological fact is often neglected in discussing the causation of delinquency. It is particularly important in connection with the ecological interpretation of crime which aims to establish a definite relationship between social behaviour and type of environment. The classical American study by Shaw and McKay (1942) shows concentrations of juvenile crime in the central and oldest districts of a number of American cities. These are generally the most dilapidated areas with the lowest rentals which are, as a rule, inhabited by the most recent immigrants. As economic status improves they tend to move out to better districts. A map of Chicago, for instance, shows that more than half the population in the central districts are either negro, or *born* in Austria, Czechoslovakia, Germany, Greece, Hungary, Italy, Ireland, Lithuania, Poland, Russia, Scandinavia, or Yugoslavia. Since that is so, it is clear that the population structure and the ensuing problems of cultural assimilation are vastly different from that in Britain. These sociological differences necessitate a different understanding of the phenomenon of delinquency. Even if a high rate of delinquency could be shown to exist in the older districts of British cities, this correlation as such would not necessarily mean that British delinquency has the same aetiology as American delinquency. As it happens, recent studies in Britain have shown that there is by no means a close correlation between dilapidated areas and criminality. Mannheim (1948) was the first to point out that in Cambridge there were concentrations of delinquency on some of the housing estates. Spencer (1954) states that the theories of the ecological school do not hold for Bristol, where there is an accumulation of social problems, including delinquency, in the outer areas of some of the new housing estates. Morris (1957) shows that in Croydon the nature of the physical environment appears to be irrelevant when considering the location of delinquency areas. The two housing estates of the interwar period with lower population densities and fairly adequate playing spaces showed higher delinquency rates than the old central areas of Croydon. Jones (1958) shows that in Leicester, too, the development of new housing estates was accompanied by a growth of delinquency on the outskirts of the town. In trying to understand the different patterns thrown up by the two countries the different sociological effects of, for instance, American immigration policy and British municipal housing policy would have to be taken into consideration.

Immigration and assimilation to new culture patterns are the keys to an understanding of life in the States and perhaps also to its pathological aberrations. The older ecological concept of a close link between social behaviour and environment has in recent years been replaced by that of normlessness or *anomie* in criminological literature. Merton (1949) sees delinquency in entirely negative terms, as the absence of a rigid behaviour pattern. He postulates that in the States 'all should strive for the same lofty goals since these are open to all'. In what way does one attain these goals? There are certain behavioural norms, some of which are a 'must', some are preferential, and some just permissive. The degree of integration and stability of a culture, he maintains, can be determined by the emphasis placed upon the behavioural norms in relation to the attainment of cultural goals. The concentration of crime in the lower strata of society is explained by the fact that there is a cultural emphasis upon material success as a final aim, but this is not accompanied by an acceptance of conventional behaviour patterns. This normlessness, or *anomie*, will bring about high delinquency rates. A similar analysis of society is used by Cohen (1956), but he arrives at a different interpretation of delinquency. Both he and Merton assume that in America there is a tendency for the individual to measure himself against everyone else in a status comparison, irrespective of social background or material circumstances. The 'lofty goals' are open to all immigrants alike, and he who does not strive to achieve them, who is not ambitious, is a social failure.

Here again the great cultural contrasts between the United States and Britain become apparent. This is the heritage of the colonizer, the adventurer who came out to build a new land, untrammelled by feudal traditions or mediaeval institutions, royalty, aristocracy, and an established church, unburdened by a life philosophy that viewed the social order as static. This is the American myth, the belief that 'any boy can be President'. Whether in actual fact social mobility is as great as it was in the days of the Frontier and of free immigration is another question, and recent studies indicate that mobility is indeed not any greater than in any of the Western European countries; but the myth still lingers. There is still considerable horizontal mobility from one place to another, and, although this does not involve a change in social status, it does bolster the feeling of unlimited opportunities, from which a rising standard of living in the affluent society does nothing to detract. Any boy may no longer be able to be President, and yet he is not permitted by his culture to shelter behind the barriers of class distinctions. He has got to be ambitious, he has got to reach for the stars.

This way of living, Cohen maintains, is an essentially middle-class one, which is based on the old Protestant virtues of industry, thrift, the development of skills, rationality, conscious planning, budgeting of time, and courteous manners. It conflicts with the working-class way of living in which the ethic of reciprocity is much stronger than that of individual responsibility. There are few aspirations with respect to jobs, and behaviour is more spontaneous and more aggressive. The working-class boy whose abilities are below the average will find it difficult to play this essentially middle-class role, and therefore will have to face continuous frustration. This drives him into building a world of his own, with its own values, in which he can make good and get the admiration, if not of his elders, at least of his peers. This is the world of the delinquent gang. The culture of the gang, Cohen maintains, is the solution to a frustration problem. In interpreting delinquency in this way Cohen differs from Merton, and he rightly points out in criticism of Merton's understanding of crime, that much of it is committed without any motivation of self-enrichment.

Stimulating as it is, this interpretation—which Cohen rightly confines to one type of delinquency only, i.e. working-class delinquency,—cannot easily be accepted in its entirety as an explanation of British working-class delinquency. Even though there may be similarities in the two countries concerning the typical middle-class and the typical working-class ways of living and the division within the working-class between the 'rough' and the 'respectable', these sub-cultural differences in each culture are not the only factors that produce frustration in its lower strata. The active working ingredient is the degree and expectation of social mobility. The experience of frustration is linked with what one thinks is expected of oneself, and what one believes to be the opportunities for advance. Britain has just emerged from a history of a very slowly growing social mobility which had its roots in a rigid class structure. Social origins, Glass says in a summary of investigations in 1954, have so far conditioned social status, and he suggests that not for another forty years or so shall we see the effects of the revolutionary expansion of educational opportunities which was introduced in the 1944 Education Act. The race is on in Britain, so to speak, and people are just beginning to wake up to it. Mogey (1956), on comparing an old-established working-class area in central Oxford with a housing estate populated by young working-class families, finds that both groups, the more go-ahead on the estate as well as the rougher type in the town centre, still show a surprising lack of aspirations for their children. 'The large number of families,' he says, 'with no real aspirations may be regarded either as a reflection of a very rudimentary knowledge of society and its opportunities, or of an extreme acceptance of a stratified society in which movement from one part to another is not particularly desired.' In an investigation of social stratification and educational opportunities in Britain and in the United States by Stephenson (1958) the interesting fact emerged that in both countries social status was an important determinant in the choice of type and amount of education in spite of a free educational system. This study does not attempt to speculate in which direction developments in the two countries are going. The fact that a free education is not the only determinant in future social position tells us little about the very subjective attitudes of those involved in the process. What do they know about the mechanisms of society, and how does such knowledge influence their aspirations? That the boys' aspirations are closely linked to their parents' attitudes and expectations has been shown by Himmelweit et al. (1952), and it is in that way that one probably gets something of a continuum and a smooth transition when new social legislation begins to operate. We must ask not only where we are, but also where we came from and where we aim to go in matters concerning social policy and its effect on individual attitudes.

Comparing the direction of developments, we might say that in the United States developments have been in the reverse. The land of unlimited opportunities has in recent years become a rigidly structured society in which achieved status is closely linked with social origin. William Whyte's 'Organization Man' is already well aware of these trends, but the masses probably still labour under the impression that the 'lofty goals' are to be reached by all. While, therefore, Cohen's interpretation of working-class delinquency appears plausible in an American setting, historical developments in Britain necessitate a different understanding.

The above considerations must not lead us to conclude that none of the work of American criminologists is of any interest to us in Britain; on the contrary, a comparison of American and British findings will enable us to elucidate parallels and variations of patterns and will help to set the questions concerning causation. These questions have to be linked with each country's social structure, and they have to be answered separately for each country. Delinquency, it is generally agreed, is but a symptom of many different underlying troubles. Area studies are important in finding the facts; and recent studies of this kind have given us a good deal of information about the social setting within which delinquency is likely to arise. There is, however, a weakness inherent in any area study, and that is the fact that any correlations of social factors that might be found to exist together with crime will not be anything other than historical information. Certain conditions of housing, employment, health, family composition, etc. may be found to exist at a certain time together with a high incidence of delinquency in any one particular place. This, important though it may be, sheds no light on the causal connectedness of any of these conditions. If the investigation is sufficiently large in scale to make such correlations statistically significant, then it may be valuable for the formulation of predictive hypotheses. Who is likely to become a delinquent in a certain social setting is the question that S. and E. Glueck have successfully answered by presenting information which was gathered during a large-scale study of an underprivileged area in Boston. Such prediction methods have been proved to be of considerable value if applied under conditions similar to those described in the initial investigation. But they cannot take the place of causal explanations; a correlation does no more than set the questions relative to an aetiology. The causal explanation that follows, on the other hand, must take into consideration the wider social framework; and it is in doing this that it becomes a specific study, an interpretation which cannot be exported to a different culture.

Let us turn to the British field of criminological studies. Ever since Burt's classical work, area studies have been carried out in various places, some of which are mentioned above (see pp. 13-15). Side by side with them individual case studies have been undertaken by sociologists, psychiatrists, or psychologists. Valuable though this approach is in shedding light on the aetiology of crime, it suffers from the handicap of a selection of case material over which the investigator has no control. The cases reach the investigator by a number of different channels. A psychiatrist might use the histories of delinquents referred to him by a juvenile court. This practice may be a frequent one in one court, and in another court only certain selected cases may be referred. The cases cannot claim to be homogeneous either in social background, or in the type of personality of the delinquent, nor can they claim to be a true sample of the full range of offenders. Again, studies of delinquent boys on probation cannot claim to deal with a true cross-section of delinquents. Grünhut (1956) has shown that ways in which juvenile courts dispose of their offenders vary considerably over the country from, for instance, Halifax, where seventy-eight per cent of young offenders are put on probation, to Swansea where only fourteen per cent are put on probation. The same applies to boys in approved schools. Cambridge sends twenty-seven per cent of its delinquents to approved schools, whereas Wigan sends only three per cent. Since the average number of boys sent to approved schools in Britain is nine per cent of all delinquents, it is questionable whether a study of boys in one of these institutions will reveal the fundamental causes of delinquency in general. Not only do disposal policies vary from one area to another, but changes in policy occur as well. The approved school population of 1960 is not of the same type as that ten years earlier, a fact which emerged during the investigations into the disturbances at Carlton Approved School (HMSO, Cmnd. 937).

The need for a new approach was voiced by Mack (1953), who demanded that investigators should undertake experimental studies 'of social behaviour, normal and aberrant, in its natural setting, the living body of society'. He emphasizes in particular the need for studying crime within the family setting. The realization that the act of law-breaking must be fitted into the set of moral beliefs prevailing in any social group has led investigators to ask: what are the moral standards of the sub-culture that is predominantly delinquency-producing? Further-more, what are the actual habits and customs of the neighbour-hood, and how far does the community live up to its professed moral standards? Mays (1954), in a study of a high-delinquency area in the Liverpool docks, found that 'Delinquency has become almost a social tradition and it is only a very few youngsters who are able to grow up in these areas without at some time or other committing illegal acts . . . Delinquency is not so much a symptom of maladjustment as of adjustment to a sub-culture in conflict with the culture of the city as a whole'. The methods and considerations of this approach are closely related to American sub-cultural investigations, and it is well worth noting that the stimulus received through American methodological experiments is immense, although this does not necessarily imply an acceptance of American interpretations.

Jephcott and Carter (1955) set out to study a high-delin-quency and a low-delinquency area in a small town near Nottingham; but on comparing certain 'black' with certain 'white' streets they eventually qualified their initial hypothesis. The comparison of areas was given up in favour of a com-parison of households within uniform neighbourhoods, and it was found that juvenile delinquency was most heavily in evidence in homes with squalid standards. These might be found in concentrations in the 'black areas' but side by side with other homes in which living standards were higher, the relationships in the family more stable, and less evidence of delinquency. The importance of this investigation lies in the fact that emphasis on the delinquency area has been narrowed down to emphasis on home conditions within the area. The questions raised by Mays in Liverpool concerning the relationship of delinquency to sub-cultural behaviour patterns could now be reformulated in the light of Jephcott and Carter's findings. Taking for granted the existence of 'delinquescent worlds,' as Professor Sprott named them (1955), we may now ask, is the pattern of deviant behaviour which is found in certain sub-cultures of such a nature that it is adopted by all youngsters whose homes have not provided a strong protection against such influences? If so, of what kind are these protections? Or on the other hand, is the home background the primary source of deviant behaviour irrespective of its neighbourhood? The survey described on the following pages attempts to shed some light on these questions.

CHAPTER II

AIMS AND METHODS OF THE SEAPORT SURVEY

THE new approach in delinquency research, as postulated by Mack (1953), suggests the study of normal and aberrant behaviour within the family and the sub-cultural setting. It may be appropriate at this point to remind the reader that the term delinquency is primarily a socio-legal concept which is closely tied up with the laws of the land. The assumption underlying delinquency research is that delinquent behaviour is deviant behaviour, and that a 'normal' person would not become a law-breaker. The motivating processes, however, that make a person a law-breaker are manifold, just as, in medical terms, the processes that create a headache are manifold. A headache may arise, for instance, from a blow on the head, from faulty eyesight, or from mental trouble. A treatise on headaches that does not differentiate headaches aetiologically is as meaningless as a treatise on delinquency that does not define the environmental setting. Human behaviour, whether normal or deviant, is social in its nature, and it can only be understood within its natural setting, as acting on and reacting to its own environment. A section of delinquent behaviour, namely that connected with organic or psychotic diseases, falls quite obviously within the medical field of reference and need not concern us here. But delinquent behaviour of a person not suffering from a tumour on the brain, a psychosis or any other mental disease that affects social behaviour, must be seen in relation to his environment. What does the delinquent's environment prescribe as 'right' and 'wrong' behaviour? Does his environment subscribe to the moral standards which are embodied in his country's legal code? If so, has it at the same time evolved a pattern of behaviour that pays lip-service to these general standards but has its own elastic methods of application? Furthermore, what do we mean by talking about a delinquent's environment: the home conditions under which he grows up and which have shaped his personality, or the sum of home conditions around his own home, his sub-culture?

Having ascertained these environmental factors we can proceed to find an understanding of the delinquent act within the delinquent's own social setting. It is obvious that the little urchin from the docks, who takes a toy from a Woolworth counter, presents an entirely different problem from, say, Peter, the adolescent delinquent boy discussed by Friedander (1947), who comes from a comfortable middle-class home. Delinquency research, therefore, should not only be carried out within the delinquent's natural setting, but it would greatly help the findings of such specific investigations if they were clad in a terminology that prevents unwarranted generalizations. The time has passed for speaking about 'fundamental causes of delinquency'; we know they do not exist.

Jephcott and Carter, as already mentioned in Chapter I, have concentrated on the type of delinquency that is found in the inadequate home. A summary of the characteristics of such a home is given in the following terms: Housekeeping conditions were permanently squalid, or only intermittent efforts were made in keeping the home clean. There was no interest in keeping up standards. Husband-wife relationships were described as extremely unstable and often irregular (e.g. indiscriminate cohabitation). Husband and wife could not be regarded as partners in the venture of family life. In the parents' relationships with their children it was found that there was often a complete disregard for them which resulted in a lack of training, and very little, if any, concern for the children's physical, spiritual, or mental welfare. Some parents might show some concern about physical dangers, such as road accidents, but they showed little interest in the children's general progress or their play-activities. They liked to give them material benefits, such as toys, but did not endeavour to provide a comfortable home. Their attitudes towards education were described as showing a complete unconcern about schooling, which resulted in leaving the decision to the children whether or not to go to school; or if the parents needed the child at home they would keep the child at home. The stark contrast of this type of inadequate home to that normally found among manual workers is obvious, and it may suffice to mention in contrast some of the characteristics found in homes which served as examples of the obverse end of Jephcott and Carter's five-point grading scheme. They were: house-proudness, the home being the centre of family life; husband-wife relationship a partnership within the family; behavioural standards which the children are taught to live up to; and emphasis on regular school attendance.

Jephcott and Carter found that detected delinquency was concentrated in these inadequate homes. They had set out to investigate a 'black' area, an area known to the police for frequent manifestations of law-breaking. They came to the conclusion that it was not the area as such, but the inadequate home in the area which was responsible. The next step for the researcher must, therefore, be an investigation of the inadequate home independent of its situation within or outside a 'black' area. If it can be demonstrated that delinquency exist in such a home, wherever that home is, and that the rate of delinquency in such a home is higher than the rate prevailing in the neighbourhood, then such evidence would show that this particular brand of delinquency is centred on the home, and not on the area. How this type of delinquency is related to the 'area-delinquescence' of John Mays is another question. It is feasible that a concentration of inadequate homes would set behaviour-patterns for the children of the neighbourhood, and that the delinquescence of an area consists of home-produced primary delinquency plus a secondary type of delinquency which, so to speak, has been caught by contagion. These and other questions it was hoped to elucidate by investigating the rate of delinquency per child at risk in families of the type described in the Nottingham survey.

For a systematic investigation of the 'inadequate' home, however, something more than the empirical approach of Jephcott and Carter is asked for. To delineate inadequacy of performance needs first of all the formulation of what constitutes an adequate performance. This is obviously a relative term which is closely linked to general standards of living. What constituted a normal performance pattern fifty years ago, does not necessarily do so in present-day society. Especially in the field of child-care the community has raised its standards considerably in recent years. An attempt had to be made, therefore, to formulate what might be considered adequacy of performance under present-day 'Welfare-State' legislation.

The social services, as embodied in this legislation, were created in a spirit of mutual assistance and care, to free society from the evils of want. The fundamental principle of welfare legislation is that living standards should not fall below a specified minimum level. Beveridge (1942), in the introduction to his social-insurance scheme which formed the basis of post-war legislation, spoke of a 'national minimum' which was to be provided by the State and which was to 'leave room and encouragement for voluntary action by each individual to provide more than that minimum for himself and his family'. The idea of providing benefits, 'in return for contributions, up to subsistence level, as of right and without means test' has been a principle which has not been attacked, although the benefits themselves have never been as high as they were envisaged by Lord Beveridge. The principle of communal responsibility for the maintenance of minimum standards of living is coupled with an increasing awareness of the need to protect those members of the community who are inherently unable to protect themselves. Such legislation extends from the care of the aged, the mentally deficient and mentally sick, to the care of children and other persons temporarily incapacitated in various ways. Legislation is supported to some extent by permissive powers of the Local Authorities, and by voluntary action.

In assessing the effects of welfare legislation, Hall (1952) expresses the fear that legislative provision of freedom from want may mould people into an accepting, passive attitude which will have a stifling effect on their personal initiative. It is interesting to notice in this and similar discussions that the universal use of the social services by those who need them is taken for granted, and the accessibility of such services to all is not questioned. The facts indicate otherwise. Why is it, for instance, that unskilled and semi-skilled workers' families make less use of child-welfare centres than the Registrar General's Class III, as stated by Spence (1954)? Why are youth clubs unable to attract the poorest sections of the community, as noted by Mays (1954)? The suitability of family planning clinics for the working-class population was questioned by Professor Madge (see Florence, 1956). But there are other considerations that have not, so far, been examined. Are, for instance, ante-natal provisions, including the supply of vitamins, fully used? Are orange juice and cod-liver oil, supplied by Local Authorities at nominal charges,* taken by all children? Is every parent aware of the fact that he has the right to apply for free school meals for his children if his income is below a certain level? Such questions are sometimes referred to in the literature concerned with so-called 'problem families' and the impression is gained that some of these services are inaccessible to the lowest strata of society.

It is often forgotten that there is a fundamental assumption which underlies the successful application of welfare services, and that is the willingness of the citizen to make full use of, and the ability of the citizen to make intelligent use of, the welfare services. Ante-natal services and general medical advice can be successful only if the patient attends regularly and carries out all instructions. The health visitor advising on the care of the baby and the young child will find her work fruitful only if she can get the mother's full co-operation. School medical inspections are of no use to those children whose parents do not encourage their regular attendance. The man on sick leave who does not apply for supplementary national assistance payments when he is eligible for them deprives his family of a minimum income.

Furthermore, the social services can be effective only if all citizens shoulder the responsibility of their own contributions —within their capabilities—in services to the community. The social services are planned and built upon the conception of a full working population and an economy that provides work for all. The National Assistance Act, 1948, under part IV of section 51 provides that the Board has power to prosecute anyone who persistently refuses or neglects to maintain himself and any person whom he is liable to maintain, and to whom in consequence assistance is given by the Board. Similarly, in the National Insurance Act, 1946, under part II of section 13, provision is made for the disqualification for six weeks from receiving unemployment benefit of anyone who left his employment without just cause, or who has lost his job through misconduct, or who has refused without good cause to apply for a

* The text reflects the position when the survey was made. Charges have since been imposed.

27

suitable job while unemployed. The right to draw unemployment benefit, therefore, is coupled with the obligation to work when the opportunity exists.

The three premises upon which welfare legislation is based appear to be the following:

(i) The State provides working opportunities for all and, through its social services, a minimum standard of living for all.

(ii) The social services are accessible to all and the active and intelligent co-operation of the consumer is assumed.

(iii) The social services are provided on the understanding that the individual is responsible for his own contribution in services to the community within his capability.

In general there is no element of compulsion in the use of the social services outside the field of education. The services are available for those who wish to use them and who are qualified to do so. Anyone who prefers to do without them may live the life he wishes to live (as long as he keeps within the law), with two exceptions. The first, the right of the Medical Officer to remove certain persons under court orders to suitable institutions to prevent injury to their own health or a nuisance to others, need not concern us here (National Assistance Act, 1948, part II, section 47). The second provision concerns the care and attention given to children and young persons. The Children and Young Persons Act, 1933, made provision for the removal of children in need of care or protection. Such children 'having . . . parents or guardians unfit to exercise care or guardianship or not exercising proper care or guardianship' can be taken from them. Whereas under this Act the prosecuting agent had to prove that neglect was wilful on the part of the parent or guardian, the Children and Young Persons (Amendment) Act, 1952, enables action to be taken in cases of neglect or ill-treatment, even when there is not sufficient evidence for the prosecution of the parent or guardian. Furthermore, under the amendment Act, it has become the duty of the local authority to investigate complaints concerning suspected neglect or ill-treatment, unless the local authority is satisfied that such an investigation is already being undertaken by another body, or that the complaint is malicious. It is this power to have enquiries made when there is a suspicion of ill-treatment or neglect that subjects the individual as parent to the scrutiny of the community. If the parents fall below certain minimum standards imposed by the community as essential for the upbringing of children, the community has the power to intervene and remove the children.

Parallel with the legislation concerning children deprived of a normal home life there has been a growing concern for the welfare of children brought up by families who are unable to manage their own affairs, but against whom there is not enough evidence to justify removal of the children. A sub-committee of the Women's Group on Public Welfare carried out a survey in association with the National Council of Social Service (1948), in which the recommendation was made that the local authority should be made responsible for providing a comprehensive service for all children living in its area, and that such a service might be combined with the care of children deprived of a normal home life. The matter was raised in Parliament twice in 1949, but the Government reached the conclusion that for the time being no additional legislation was required, and that by fully co-ordinating the existing statutory and voluntary services the welfare of children in their own homes would be fully safeguarded. In a joint circular from the Home Office, the Ministry of Health, and the Ministry of Education (1950), all local authorities were asked to ensure that such co-ordination of services existed, and the appointment by each local authority of a designated officer was advocated. This officer was to be responsible for such co-ordination and its efficient application. The Seventh Report on the Work of the Children's Department (1955) stated that of the 123 designated officers appointed by that date 56 were Children's Officers, 39 Medical Officers, 23 Clerks of Council, 4 Chief Education Officers, and 1 was a member of a Council. The periodic meetings called by the designated officers to consider cases are usually attended by representatives of the local authority's children's, health, education, housing, and welfare departments, and of the National Assistance Board and the probation service. Such representation, however, varies from one local authority to another; in Seaport, for instance, representatives of the children's, welfare, and probation departments attend only when certain cases in which they are already involved are on the agenda. In addition there may be representation of voluntary organizations. The Seventh Report mentions that in some areas only the National Society for the Prevention of Cruelty to Children is included, whereas in others there are also representatives from the Council of Social Service, the Diocesan Moral Welfare Association, the Salvation Army, Family Service Units, Women's Voluntary Services, Women's Institutes, the Family Welfare Association, and other adult and youth organizations.

It is this co-ordination committee which normally deals with families who have been referred to it for suspected child neglect, and sometimes for suspected ill-treatment. Some consideration concerning the meaning of the words neglect and ill-treatment become necessary at this point. In the before-mentioned report by the Women's Group on Public Welfare these concepts are considered at some length. The report was based on evidence from three sources: a study of mothers in Holloway prison serving sentences for child neglect; a study of widowed mothers; and a study of cases from Dr Barnardo's Homes. Evidence was also given by a number of experts directly concerned with the problem of neglect. A definition of cruelty and neglect was offered in the following passage:

We have distinguished between wilful or intentional cruelty and the kind of neglect which, though it may amount to cruelty in its effects, is yet unintentional, though none the less damaging to the child on that account. Cruelty has been taken to mean throughout deliberate physical ill-treatment. Neglect has been interpreted widely as failure to make adequate provision for the physical, emotional, and intellectual needs of a child. Affection and security are the two most important non-material needs of a child, and the gross failure to provide these has been regarded as an indication of neglect as culpable as failure to provide food and warmth. The parents' refusal to avail themselves of communal services for children such as educational opportunities or medical care has been considered as also culpable.

In a joint report issued by the British Medical Association and the Magistrates' Association in 1956 on 'Cruelty to, and Neglect of Children', evidence from a large number of individuals and associations concerned with the prevention of neglect was collated, and the following definition of cruelty and neglect was offered:

Cruelty and neglect are not easily definable separately. In general they constitute treatment as a result of which a child's potential development is retarded or completely suppressed by mental, emotional, and/or physical suffering produced as the outcome of a deprivation of minimum requirements. Physical cruelty and neglect are often accompanied by mental cruelty which includes—
(i) the effect on the child's mind of constant exposure to domestic strain, immoral behaviour, insecurity, and anxiety;
(ii) deliberate actions on the part of the parents or guardians which are calculated to frighten the child excessively or reduce him to an unbearable state of mental or emotional tension;
(iii) the denial of adequate affection or means of self-expression.

The emphasis in the Women's Group's publication is on the difference between intentional and unintentional ill-treatment of the child, whereas the Joint Report states that cruelty or neglect cannot easily be treated separately, and that both forms of ill-treatment may be equally damaging in their psychological effects on the child. The latter conclusion was also arrived at by the Women's Group, and it was for that reason that a change in the law was advocated which was eventually incorporated into the 1952 Amendment Act.

The key phrases of the two reports are 'failure to make adequate provision for the physical, emotional, and intellectual needs of a child' and 'deprivation of minimum requirements [necessary for] a child's potential development' respectively. Although the authors of both reports stress the equal importance of physical and emotional deprivation and anxieties caused by emotional tensions, it appears to me on the available evidence that co-ordination committees are primarily concerned with the prevention of neglect of a child's material needs. For instance, in a report submitted in 1951 by the Medical Officer of Health in Seaport to the Co-ordination Committee, the needs of sixty-five families referred by health visitors are summed up in the following five categories:

'(1) cleanliness of persons as well as things,

(2) clothing,
(3) bedding,
(4) food (the priority need of this would probably be higher if it were not for school feeding),
(5) furniture.'

It must, however, be remembered that the physical neglect of a child inevitably has emotional repercussions; and the primary emphasis on the failure to provide minimum material requirements does not mean, therefore, that the emotional needs of the child have been entirely overlooked. Deprivation of affection on the other hand, and emotional ill-treatment, may also occur in families who live in relative material comfort; but such cases, although they may be known to a Children's Officer, would not normally be referred to a co-ordination committee as the services of its component bodies are not required in such cases.

We have so far established that, outside the field of education, the use of the social services is not obligatory, but that they need the active and intelligent co-operation of the consumer to be effective. In addition, the community enforces a certain minimum standard of living for its children. There are, therefore, certain limitations to deviant, although not unlawful, behaviour. These limitations affect three different aspects of family life. They are (i) financial solvency, (ii) health, and (iii) education.

(i) A policy of full employment and social security for temporary loss of work implies that a man who is willing to work and who has enough foresight to budget his income will always be solvent. Failure in this respect is coupled with social sanctions of various kinds. For instance, if a person contracts a debt and does not carry out the conditions of repayment imposed on him by court order, he may be sent to prison. Again, failure to pay the rent may lead to eviction. Or again, bankruptcy proceedings impose certain obligations and limitations on further activities.

(ii) Provisions made through the National Health Service Act enable every individual to live healthily, and demand of every individual certain minimum standards of hygiene. The Medical Officer of Health has the power, under a court order, to remove persons who suffer from grave chronic disease, or live in insanitary conditions, or are unable to devote to themselves proper care, to suitable institutions. Again, the physical neglect of children may lead to the prosecution of the parents, or the removal of the children.

(iii) The principles underlying universal education, established in 1870, with its concomitant compulsory-attendance laws, passed in 1876, have been operative for so long that they are generally and unquestionably accepted. Non-attendance of children at school will result either in prosecution of the parents or in bringing the child himself before the juvenile court, and may result in supervision by a probation officer, or in severe cases removal from home.

Families who continuously or for lengthy periods fall short of any requirements outlined under the heading of solvency, health, and education, will sooner or later come to the notice of the local authorities as potential or suspected cases of child-neglect. They exhibit a number of indices or symptoms which are easily recognizable by the observer. These deficiencies in various fields of activity may be likened to symptoms in the medical field; the appearance of a rash, a headache, and a high temperature will indicate the existence of one or another illness. Again, as in the medical field, these social symptoms may appear in various groupings. Some families show a preponderance of symptoms of inadequacy in a range of activities linked with income; others develop such symptoms primarily in the field of health and hygiene, as expressed in general housekeeping standards. Again, it may be the attitude to education and the social services in general that creates the primary difficulty. None of the symptoms by itself would suffice to draw the attention of the local authority to such a family, but a combination of a number of such symptoms would in all likelihood make out the family as a social nuisance. None of the symptoms as such would give an indication of the underlying characteristics of the family, and the causes of these deficiencies are manifold. The primary interest of the local authority is the fact that child-neglect is in evidence; what caused it is a secondary consideration.

These general considerations of what might be considered to be 'performance-inadequacy' under present-day legislation in Britain formed a basis for a method by which the case material of the present survey was collected so as to provide a homogeneous group suitable for a sociological investigation. The willingness of the Local Authority to put its files at my disposal offered an opportunity of investigating a group of families whose living-standards are similar to those described by Jephcott and Carter. These families had been referred to the Medical Officer of Health, who is Chairman of the local Co-ordination Committee, as showing evidence of child-neglect. An investigation of this group of families satisfies a number of methodological stipulations:

(i) The case material was drawn from all areas of the city and was not confined to certain high-delinquency areas.

(ii) The referral agents do not include any officials dealing with delinquency. The object of the Co-ordination Committee is prevention of child-neglect, not the treatment of delinquency.

(iii) The case material at my disposal consisted of the total intake during a specified period.

(iv) It is a survey of families chosen for their sociological characteristics, and not a survey of families exhibiting delinquency.

The aims of the survey were the following. It was hoped in the first place to find out whether this group of families is the breeding ground of delinquency, after allowing for the fact that because of their high fertility there would be relatively more children at risk. The rate of delinquency per child at risk was to be compared with that prevailing in the neighbourhoods. It was hoped, secondly, to compare the families with delinquent children with other families in the research group without delinquent children. Any characteristics held by one group and not the other might shed valuable light on causation. In the third place it was hoped to find out the connection between juvenile delinquency and parental criminality.

The cases referred to the Co-ordination Committee during the first three years of its existence form the material upon which the survey is based. As previously pointed out, one of the requirements for delinquency research is a sociological homogeneity of the case material, and it was soon apparent that the 157 cases which were passed on to me did not possess a uniform character. Ford, Thomas, and Ashton (1955) had already pointed out in a report of the work of the Southampton Co-ordination Committee that there was a disadvantage in using for research purposes case material that had been collected for administrative purposes. In Seaport, as in Southampton, no clear definition of what constituted child-neglect was supplied to the referral agents. In Seaport, again as in Southampton, cases were referred to the Committee by various individuals, belonging to various statutory or voluntary agencies, who would all approach the problem from their own specific angles. It was imperative, therefore, to make a selection of cases of a sociologically more homogeneous character upon which a criminological investigation could be based.

On the basis of the general considerations concerning performance-inadequacy in the Welfare State a symptom-analysis sheet was composed for each family on which a number of performance-inadequacy symptoms could be entered as observed over a period of five years. The symptoms chosen were of such a nature that by careful observation and corroboration of information from reliable sources they could easily be ascertained. All symptoms are taken from the field of performance, and none are of the nature of personality defects or other possible causes of performance-inadequacy. They are, in fact, the current deficiencies which were found singly, or in various combinations, among the families referred to the Co-ordination Committee. Grouped under the headings of solvency, health, and education, the indices chosen are the following:

A. Solvency.
   1. Father has a bad work record.
   2. Father deprives mother of part of his income; shortage of housekeeping money; mother bad manager.
   3. Rent arrears.
   4. Other debts.
   5. House scantily equipped.
   6. Shortage of children's clothing, especially shoes.
B. Health.
   7. Children are sent dirty to school.
   8. Children are verminous or nitty.
   9. House dirty and smelly.
   10. Mother cooks not at all or very little.
C. Education.
   11. Bad school attendance.

It was decided to include in the research set all families who showed a certain minimum number of the above symptoms. An analysis-sheet was prepared for each family on which were entered information and observations for the five-year period 1952-56. These sheets contain information from all local authority departments who had had dealings with the family, the employment exchange, the youth employment bureau, and the National Assistance Board. Whenever possible, other agencies were also consulted. (See Appendix I.) The sheets incorporated some of the information obtained by personal interview with health visitors and teachers. (See Appendix II.) Whenever factual information was involved it was corroborated when necessary. In cases of assessments, the statements of at least two workers acquainted with the family were taken. In addition, I conducted a personal interview with all families so as to obtain a uniform overall impression. In this way the work record of the father was first checked at the Labour Exchange, and cross-checked, when possible, in the local-authority housing department by consulting the periodic wages declarations that are required in Seaport for the operation of a rent-rebate scheme. Information about cleanliness of children, the house, and the mother's ability to cook was obtained in the interviews with health visitors and social workers. In the interviews with the teachers such information was also supplied incidentally in many cases, although the primary object of these interviews was the ascertainment of educational attainments. School attendance was checked in the education department by working out the average attendance over two terms for each child. Definitions of the terms used, such as 'bad work record' or 'bad school attendance' are supplied in the following chapters describing the case material.

Only such symptoms as had been observed for a lengthy period, i.e. well over a year, were recorded so as to exclude temporary deterioration of living conditions caused by some crisis such as illness of the mother. To some extent this is taken for granted by the referral agents of the co-ordination committee. It was found, however, that a considerable number of families had been only in temporary difficulties when referred, and they were, therefore, excluded from the final research group. As a check on the allotment of marks it was decided to add to the symptom analysis sheet the final item:

12. Formal case opened by the National Society for the Prevention of Cruelty to Children.

Such cases are opened only after the NSPCC inspector has convinced himself that there is actual or potential danger of child-neglect or ill-treatment, and a case is very unlikely to be opened when a family has an inadequate performance only because of temporary bad fortune. The total possible score for inadequacies of performance was thus twelve.

The analysis sheet covers, as mentioned above, the five years 1952-1956. The rather long period was chosen for a double purpose. It was found that in some cases detailed information was available only for a period before the beginning of the investigation. Certain cases had come to the notice of the Co-ordination Committee during a particular crisis, and had been deleted when this was dealt with. Other cases had been deleted because the Committee felt unable to deal with them and decided to postpone further consideration until a specialized team of workers was available. (It was hoped at the time that a Family Service Unit would be set up in Seaport.) In other cases, again, it was found that the problems of an earlier period had cleared up naturally through the years: no further children were born, the mother's health improved, the youngest children entered school and gave the mother more time to cope with housework, and the oldest children were perhaps beginning to earn and add to the family income. Within the research set itself there turned out to be two types, both of which showed the necessary minimum number of performance-inadequacy symptoms. One group showed these symptoms clearly on the left of the analysis sheet during the early years of the five-year period (which also were the first five years of the co-ordination committee), and they showed definite signs of improvement during more recent years. The other group showed its heaviest markings on the right side of the sheet and could therefore be considered current cases.

It was not always possible to get information on every item. It was, for instance, particularly difficult to get reliable information on the mother's cooking habits. Similarly, statements about debts were sometimes made in the personal interview with the father or mother which could not be corroborated. Three families were no longer visited by either health visitors or social workers. The information obtained in these cases was scanty, but the impression was gained during the personal interview that they should be included in the research set. Apart from these three families, only those scoring at least five marks for performance inadequacy at any one time were included in the research set. The maximum actually scored by any family was eleven out of the possible twelve.

By this process a great many families which had been referred to the co-ordination committee were eliminated. The original total case load consisted of 157 families. Of these forty-seven families had moved, or had been broken up, or could not be traced before the personal interview took place, and they were, therefore, not included in the investigation. This left 110 families. Information was gathered concerning all these, and all were visited by me. Performance inadequacies were recorded on the symptom analysis sheets, and on this basis fifty-two families were finally chosen to form the research set. This fifty-two included the three families mentioned before for whom available information was scanty; forty-nine scored five or more symptoms of performance-inadequacy at any one particular period. It must be remembered, however, that this does not constitute the total case load of this type of families in Seaport at the present time. For purposes of this survey, only cases referred to the co-ordination committee up to January, 1955, have been considered, and many have been referred since that date.

As has been postulated earlier, by this method a certain homogeneity of the group was obtained, based on an analysis of performance-inadequacy. Although it is clear that the causes of these inadequacies are many and are likely to vary from case to case, it can be stated with some confidence that the scale used for the measurement of the performance standards of each family is a clearly defined one, and that a certain objectivity of measurement was obtained. It may be argued that the standards set for inclusion in the research group are either too high or too low; to a large extent this will depend on subjective judgment. The present investigation is, however, not concerned with questions of this nature. The purpose of defining the group by this method is not a diagnostic one, nor is the method necessarily suitable for use in the field of social work. Its only purpose has been to obtain a homogeneous group of families suitable for an investigation of juvenile delinquency.

CHAPTER III

THE PARENTS

AS might be expected in a study of cases whose only common factor is performance-inadequacy, the variety of family patterns exhibited by the fifty-two cases is so great that it appears an impossible task to describe the patterns in a way that does not blur the characteristics. Not only do the personalities of the parents vary widely, not only are their physical, mental, and emotional make-up as untypical as in any other loosely-formed group in society; but also the combinations of parental characters form such a varied matrimonial pattern that the impact of events is bound to create widely differing experiences. In the final analysis it is, of course, the attitude of the parents in tackling life in the set of living conditions in which they find themselves which determines success or failure for them. This study of fifty-two families cannot concern itself with the psychiatric implications of the sociological observations recorded in it; all it can do is to sum up the sociological observations in such a way that psychiatric interpretation becomes possible. Ideally, a study of this nature ought to be carried out simultaneously by workers in both disciplines.

The sociological information that has been gathered about the families will be presented under the headings of parents, children, housing, and behaviour patterns. This will be followed by a discussion of the juvenile delinquency found among them. Since a mere statistical presentation in percentage groupings of individual factors will not convey the complex living patterns of each family, such presentation will be given only in relevant contexts. It is a statistical fact, for example, that 27 per cent of the fathers had good work records and 38 per cent had long periods of unemployment, but this information is unenlightening unless it is coupled with the father's health record, with the mother's ability at home-making with limited resources, and with the size of the family. The statistical information which may be of interest in contexts other than the main theme of this book is presented in the appendix. The text focuses on correlations that appear significant, not only statistically but in the human sense, and endeavours to interpret these correlations. Case histories will be given as illustrations.

1. HEALTH AND WORK RECORDS OF THE PARENTS

The most decisive factor in determining the well-being of a family is perhaps the father's earning capacity. If this is impaired, the additional strain put on the mother's capacities may be such that she finds herself unable to cope. In this sense of providing the material necessities for the family the father is the first line and the mother the second line of defence. It was most important, therefore, to obtain an accurate assessment of the fathers' work records. These records were assessed under three headings, as good, indifferent, or bad, on the basis of information supplied by the various agencies (listed in the appendix) to whom the parents were known. If the records showed a relatively uninterrupted work rhythm with only occasional periods out of work, caused by sickness or other defined reasons, the father's work record was classified as good. If, on the other hand, he was found to have exhausted the period of unemployment benefit and to have been on National Assistance for over one year, his work record was classified as bad. Intermediate cases were termed indifferent, and fell into the following categories.

(i) Frequent changes of jobs, interspersed with lengthy periods of unemployment, or prison sentences, or loss of unemployment benefit because of refusal to accept a suitable job.

(ii) Part-time work only, with periods of unemployment.

(iii) Unemployment for periods of a year or more, but working at the time of the survey.

Table I shows that there were 14 fathers with good records, 14 fathers with indifferent records, and 20 fathers with bad records. Two families had no father, one because of divorce, the other because of death.

Since only 29 per cent of the working fathers had a good work record, we were led to ask what reason there was, if any,

Table I.

Correlation of father's health and work record.

	Good	Indifferent	Bad	Old Age Pensioner	Total
Health		Work record			
Normal	2 4 9 11 17 19 31 48 49 50	1 3 37	—	32 36	15
Disabled	—	6 28	5 12 21 25 34 39 41 45 46	—	11
Accident	—	14 16 26	—	—	3
Ill-health	20 22 29	8 23 35 38 42	7 27 30 33	—	12
TB	—	43	—	—	1
Mentally deficient	15	—	—	—	1
Mentally ill	—	—	10 13 18 24 40 44 47	—	7
Dead (case 51)	—	—	—	—	1
Divorced (case 52)	—	—	—	—	1
Totals	14	14	20	2	52
Per cent of those working	29	29	42	—	

Footnote. The numbers in italics are case code numbers.

for over two-thirds of the group to be out of work so frequently and in some cases permanently. Information about their health revealed that all the men with a bad work record suffered from some disability: nine are registered as disabled at the unemployment exchange. Another seven, although not so registered, have at one time or another suffered from mental illness for which they have had treatment (with the exception of one, who was, however, twice convicted for attempting suicide). The remaining four suffer from chronic ill-health. The fourteen men who had indifferent work records were also mostly disabled in one way or another; two of them had actually registered as disabled at the employment exchange. Three others had had accidents which had affected their physique, but they preferred not to be registered as disabled, as they felt it prejudiced their prospects. One of them suffered from dormant tuberculosis, and another five had various chronic ailments. (Diagnostic details are listed in Appendix III.) Only three men out of this group with indifferent work records were classified as of normal health. We will discuss their problems later on.

Table II.

Correlation of father's work record and mother's health.

Mother's health	Good	Indifferent			Bad		Old Age Pensioner	Total
		Father's Work record						
Normal	2 9 17	1	8	16	13	21	—	26
	20 22 29	23	35	37	24	25		
	48 50	38	42		30	33		
					34	39		
					44	45		
Ill-health	11 19 31	14	28		5	7	—	12
					10	40		
					41	46		
					47			
Mentally retarded	15 49	3	6	26	27		32 36	8
Mentally ill	4	43			18		—	3
Dead	—	—			12		—	1
Totals	14	14			20		2	50*

*One father dead and one divorced make the total up to 52 families.

Case 51 widowed mother of normal health.

Case 52 divorced mother mentally ill.

Footnote. The numbers in italics are case code numbers.

The men who were regular workers, on the other hand, were mostly reasonably fit. Only three had some ailment; one of them suffered from nephritis, the other two from gastric ulcers. There was also a borderline mentally deficient man in this group.

On looking at the mothers' health records (Table II) we found that on the whole they were healthier than the fathers. Half of the group appeared to be of normal health and not abnormal intelligence. Twelve suffered from chronic physical illnesses, four had had treatment for mental illness, and a further eight

Table III.

Correlation of father's work record with size of family.

Number of children	Good	Indifferent	Bad	Old Age Pensioner	Total
		Work record			
3	—	—	45 46	—	2
4	—	—	18	—	1
5	11	38 42	44	32	5
6	31 49	3 6 14 23 43	7 13 21 24 25	—	12
7	19 22	26 28 37	5 33 47	36	9
8	4 20	35	—	—	3
9	—	8 16	10 27 34	—	5
10	15 17 29	—	12 39	—	5
11	2 9 48 50	1	30 41	—	7
12	—	—	40	—	1
Totals	14	14	20	2	50*

*One father dead and one divorced make the total up to 52 families.

Footnote. The numbers in italics are case code numbers.

were mentally retarded, one of these was known to the local authority as a borderline mental defective. (Illnesses of the mothers are listed in Appendix IV.)

The comparatively large proportion of mothers with normal health poses the question: is there some other disabling factor that might provide a clue to the mother's inability to cope? Ten mothers were married to disabled men who have been out of work for a long time. One was bringing up a family as a widow. Eight had husbands who were irregular workers, mostly owing to disabilities. But there was a group of mothers of normal health whose husbands were regular workers; were there any other particular difficulties that these women had to face? An important factor, closely linked with the mother's general health and ability to manage the family, is the number of her pregnancies and their frequency. A mother may enjoy good health and yet be so frequently incapacitated by confinements and so overburdened with the care of young children that her general faculties become impaired. Furthermore, the larger the family, the lower the income per head, a fact that is of vital importance in low income groups. It was not practicable to ascertain the frequency of pregnancies, but the number of surviving children was more readily obtainable. As would be expected, this increased with the age of the mother, being 5.4 children for mothers aged 20—29 (of whom there were five), 5.9 children for mothers aged 30—34 (of whom there were thirteen), and 8.3 children for those aged 35 or older (of whom there were thirty-four). The average number of children for the whole group is 7.4, and thirteen families have ten or more children. The national average number of children per family over the last thirty years has been just over two; this contrast shows the considerably greater burden that the mothers from the research set have to carry in bringing up their families. Table III relates the size of the family to the father's work record.

On correlating the mother's health with the father's work record and the size of the family, we got at least a partial answer to the question concerning the mother's inability to cope. We found that in families where the father's work record is good, and the mother's health is normal, the number of children is higher than the average for the group. There are six families with more than ten children, and another two families with seven and eight respectively. In the groups of families where the fathers have bad or indifferent work records, this correlation of size of family with mother's health is not apparent. One might conclude from this that the main disabling factor for these healthy mothers with steady incomes is an unusually large family; disabling, of course, because the incomes are low. We come back to this later when we discuss incomes.

Having obtained a general picture, let us now consider in greater detail the three groups of men with good, indifferent, and bad work records. What can we learn from comparing their work records with their wives' health and general capacities, taking into account the number of children they have to bring up?

A. Men with good work records

There are fourteen fathers who are steady workers. One is a borderline mental defective who has, however, managed to hold down a job for many years. He is married to a mentally-defective woman, and they have ten children. An exact classification cannot be made of the degree of mental deficiency. Both parents had attended special schools for educationally subnormal children and both were known to the public Health Department. That they have been able to carry on, although (as will be revealed later on) not very successfully, was possible only because six of their children have been at residential special schools at one time or another. Another three men have chronic ailments, but as their wives are all healthy, they have been able to keep reasonably steady work records. They are bringing up families of seven, eight, and ten children. The remaining ten men are of normal health. Five of these have wives suffering from some disability; one wife is mentally ill, one retarded, and three have physical ailments. The wives of the other five men are of normal health, but we have already pointed out that they have the largest families: one has ten, the other four have eleven children. As will be shown later, these families are trying to bring up their children on an income that is generally below subsistence level; and it is therefore perhaps not surprising that they find themselves included in the research set.

It appears then that this group of steady workers is handicapped either by ill-health, physical or mental, or by an unusually large size of family coupled with a very low income-capacity.

B. Men with indifferent work records

There are fourteen men with irregular working habits. Of these, as mentioned before, eight are registered as disabled, and it is difficult for them to get suitable work. Another three had accidents which had interrupted their work and diminished their capacity. There are only three men in this group who enjoy normal health. A short account of their histories will give an indication of the variety and complexity of conditions that may induce a man of apparently good physical health to adopt an irregular work pattern. To facilitate comparison with the statistical information given in the Appendices, the men's code numbers have been added to the text.

The first case (code number 1) is a general labourer, who has mainly been working on building sites, and lately as a boiler scaler in the docks. This particular employment is of an irregular nature, as there is not always work available. But even as a general labourer in the building industry this man had lengthy periods of unemployment; normally, however, he got back to work before his unemployment benefit expired. His health is considered to be good by the health visitor and the child care officer. The man himself confirmed this in an interview with me. His wife, too, is of normal health. They have eleven children, not all of whom are at home. At the time of the investigation there were seven children under fifteen living with the parents. This man, when working on building sites, would bring home about £10 in the season if a full week is worked; in the winter however he would have considerable periods of unemployment. His total spendable income after deduction of insurance payments and fares while in work has been some £9 plus £2 18s—in family allowances. While out of work he would get from unemployment plus national assistance payments* a total of £11 12s—plus full payment of rent. It is the practice of the National Assistance Board to assess each case individually. It is obvious from this example, however, that this man is not much

* The rates quoted refer to those in force since March, 1961.

better off financially while in work than when he is unemployed. It is likely that in this case the National Assistance Board would make a deduction from his allowances, a practice which will be discussed more fully further on, so that this man, while out of work, would have some five to ten shillings less than he would normally have in spending money while working. The inducement of an extra ten shillings or so while in work is not always great enough to balance the additional costs incurred by going to work, such as fares, meals out, wear and tear on clothes, etc. Family budgets will be examined in greater detail further down, and it may suffice to say here that for a large family an unskilled labourer's wage plus family allowances is not sufficient to raise the family above subsistence level, and that such a position may easily lead to voluntary periods of unemployment.

The second case (code number 3) presents a different problem. This man, although also of normal health, is inclined to suffer from bronchial trouble in the winter and has been known to take days off so that his pay packet has hardly ever been a full week's wage during the off-season. His wife is described by health visitor and social worker as somewhat mentally retarded. They have six children. Since this man has been known to be somewhat irregular, he has also always been among the first to be dismissed and has had considerable periods of unemployment. His wife, who has not been able to cope with a growing family, has had some support on and off from various agencies, but owing to frequent changes in personnel dealing with her no headway was made. Conditions deteriorated, rent arrears mounted, and other debts accumulated. When the father found himself in prison for non-payment of a court order on furniture, his attitude to work changed entirely, and after discharge he became actively unwilling to find work.

The third case (code number 37) presents yet another problem. This man, too, is a general labourer. He was nineteen years old when the war broke out, and he served in the army for six years. After discharge he could not settle down to steady employment and he developed a very irregular work pattern. During 1954, for instance, he had seventeen different jobs with periods of unemployment in between. He was married straight after discharge from the Army, and the first child was born in

1946. In 1951 he was convicted for neglecting his four children and was sent to prison for three months. The children were committed to the care of the local authority, and the father has since spent several further terms in prison for non-payment of maintenance orders. In the course of this he has become more difficult about finding work as he is not assessed by the Children's Department while unemployed. Unemployment benefit was disallowed once for six weeks because he refused without good reason to accept a job. He has since had another three children.

It is obvious that the problems presented by these three families are of a very different nature. The implications of this will be discussed further on, and it may suffice to say at this point that the reason for an irregular work record is by no means always due to one fundamental personality trait.

C. *Men with bad work records*

This group, comprising twenty men, is the largest of the three. They are all disabled in some way, and they need less explaining in terms of additional handicaps than men of good health. Half of these men, however, have an additional handicap in the form of a wife who is suffering from ill-health, or who is mentally ill, or mentally retarded. One man is a widower who is bringing up ten children, himself chronically disabled by bronchial trouble.

2. TYPE OF WORK AND INCOMES

A. *General discussion*

The following information is based primarily on data collected at the Ministry of Labour and the National Assistance Board. The facts concerning labour conditions and rates of pay refer to 1961. The figures for incomes are approximate minimum and maximum amounts. It was considered preferable to present the family incomes in this way, rather than to rely entirely on the statements made by the parents during the interview. The information given during the interview has been incorporated into Chapter VI.

Most men in the research set of families have not learnt any particular trade. Their wages could not, therefore, be expected to be higher than the lowest industrial wages. An unskilled factory labourer who has no chance of bonus payments or overtime work earns around £8 10s 0d per week, which means that he brings home about eight pounds after deduction of the national insurance contribution. Most men in the survey were of the type that would not get much opportunity for extra earnings like a bonus, overtime work, or priced jobs. Such extras are usually offered only to men who are reasonably steady and regular.

An unskilled labourer working in the building industry at the rate of 4s 10½d per hour would be able to make £10 4s 9d for a week of 42 hours in the season. In the winter, if no indoor work is available on the building sites, there is a tendency to unemployment. While conditions in the building industry were good until about 1956, only a good labourer has been able to remain in regular employment since then. The labouring jobs on British Railways are slightly more advantageous; although the rate is not high for labourers—£8 8s 0d per week—there is usually an opportunity to make up with overtime, night duty, and weekend work. Some of the men in the research set have worked for British Railways at times, but only two have had a continuous record of railway employment. The majority of the unskilled men have been working in factories, on building sites, or as fruit hawkers, dustmen, cellarmen, warehouse porters, etc. These men, when in work, have not a great chance to make more than £9 per week, and they are more likely to make about £8 10s 0d. After deduction of National Insurance payments they have about £8 to £8 10s 0d at their disposal. There are altogether forty men in this group.

Eight of the fathers had learnt a trade or acquired some skills that would enable them to bring in higher earnings. Three of them, however, have been unemployed for a considerable period. One is an upholsterer who has been the victim of the ups and downs of his trade. He worked on his own account for a number of years, then failed, and was subsequently employed in a furniture shop. The trade is very seasonal, and there has been considerable local unemployment in recent years. As more of the local furniture stores are acquired by large national firms, upholsterers become increasingly redundant. Another man is a shoe repairer. He is crippled, and generally known to be a difficult man of an aggressive type. He has not been able to hold down a job, and has been unemployed for several years. The third man was working part-time as a slaughterman during the early stages of the survey. He suffered from heart disease, and had to give up work. He has died recently.

The five remaining semi-skilled or skilled men have the following trades:

(i) Brushmaker. This man's eyesight has deteriorated gradually, and he is now registered as partially sighted. He has recently been employed in the Blind Institute's workshop, where he earns £9 9s 0d per week.

(ii) Painter and decorator. The rate per hour in this trade is 5s 6d. In the summer there is usually opportunity for some overtime work, but the trade is very dependent on the weather. During the winter there has recently been considerable local unemployment.

(iii) Baker. The minimum rate per hour is 3s 10d with a fifteen per cent increase for night work. Again, it is difficult to estimate the weekly earnings; they would certainly not be less than £11 and possibly as much as £13.

(iv) and (v). Two men are steel erectors. The minimum time rate is 5s 4d per hour. In this trade price work in the form of sub-contracting is often done. It is for that reason difficult to guess the average weekly earnings of these men, but they are likely to be not less than £14.

B. Incomes of men with good work records

There are only fourteen men with good work records in the group, which means that in only fourteen of the fifty-two households is a regular pay packet brought home. Four of them are the above-mentioned men with special skills; the brushmaker is not included as his work record was very irregular until he joined the Blind Institute's workshop. The painter's average earnings are difficult to estimate correctly. He is a council house tenant and occupies a house with a weekly rent of £1 12s 6d. As no rebate was allowed and as he has seven children under sixteen years old, it is likely that his average earnings are above £14 10s 0d per week during employment, but they are not likely to be much higher. The family allowances of £2 18s 0d would in this case roughly cover expenses on rent and light and fuel; which would leave some £1 8s od per head for food, clothing, household expenditure and all other incidentals. This it may be argued, does not leave much margin; the aggravating circumstances in this case, however, appeared in the form of another woman who was regularly taken out by the father and who considerably strained the budget. The baker's weekly earnings may be in the region of £11 10s od after deduction of insurance payments; since he has been allowed a rent rebate of 8s od it is improbable that his average earnings are much higher. He has eight children for whom he gets £3 8s od in family allowances. He pays £1 5s 10d as rent. On the estimate that he would need about £1 5s od to £1 10s od per week for light and fuel, his family is left with some £12 for ten people. The two steel erectors are probably the highest income earners in the research set; it is likely that they earn not less than £14 on the average. Both have families of eleven children each. In one case they were all under fifteen when the survey was carried out, and this man paid a rebated rent of £1 6s 10d. His family allowances were £4 18s od. Rent, light, fuel, and insurance would take about £3, which leaves this family with some £16 for thirteen people. The other man had two boys of working age which made calculations more difficult, but it appeared that material shortages were not as great as in the family all of whose children were still at school.

These skilled men apart, the remaining ten labourers are not likely to earn more than £9 per week; probably they are nearer the minimum of about £8 10s od per week, if they work a full week. In the course of the investigation I got the impression that there was a fairly heavy incidence of short absences from work through minor accidents, though it was not possible to make a systematic study of this. The many bad-luck stories which the parents told me during the interview could not always be corroborated, and may in a good few cases have been just an excuse for a day away from work. In some cases, however, the injury that caused the absence was obvious; in other cases there was evidence of accidents in some official file. The impression that these men are peculiarly prone to accidents has been confirmed by other workers who are acquainted with this type of man. Hersey (1952), in a study of workers in the United States and Germany, found that out of 400 minor accidents more than half took place when the worker was in a worried, apprehensive, or other low emotional state. The foremost causes were plant worries, home difficulties, fatigue, and lack of sleep, or periodic emotional disturbance. It is very likely that the three last-mentioned causes offer an explanation for the accident-proneness that seems apparent in the research group. Whatever the reason, however, for not working a full week, there was a good deal of evidence that the men did not always bring home a full pay packet. The reasons given during the interview ranged from accidents at work, minor ailments, and heavy colds, to minding the children while the wife was laid up. The latter explanation is, I believe, of great significance in this group, as they are isolated families who have very little, if any, support from their kin. A day or two at home away from work does not necessarily lead to the loss of the job, but it does mean a day or two of lost earnings. This loss cannot be made up by claiming sickness benefit, if sickness is the cause, since such a claim cannot be made for a period shorter than three days, and benefit is only allowed for the first three days of sickness when the total period off work exceeds twelve days.

It is, however, of interest to examine the financial position of these men in relation to family size and rent in the weeks when they have a full pay packet. The actual budget of each family depends on a number of variables, of which the age of the children and the ensuing family allowances are important. As family allowances are paid out for children under sixteen irrespective of age, the most difficult stage for the parents is that of the growing school child. When the children leave school and start employment, the usual pattern is that they give their mother a contribution of about a pound to thirty shillings a week and relieve her of the responsibility for their clothes. In general it can be said that the greater the number of children in a family, the more precarious becomes the financial position. Family allowances are not paid for the first child, and the present allowance for the second child is eight shillings per week, with ten shillings for the third and subsequent children. The theoretical basis for the payment of such allowances out of taxation is fully argued in the Beveridge Report on Social Insurance and Allied Services (1942), and it is emphasized that without such payments no satisfactory system of social security could be established. It is obvious, however, that family allowances do not cover subsistence expenses. If the rates payable for children by the National Assistance Board in 1961 are taken as a minimum for covering subsistence needs, the family allowance of 10s 0d falls short of them by 7s 0d for a child under five, by 10s 0d for a child aged 5—11, and by 14s 0d for a child aged 11—16.

For an unskilled labourer, earning on the average £8 10s 0d per week, with eight children, it is hardly possible, even with careful management, to raise the standard of living above subsistence level. He would get a total of £3 8s 0d in family allowances. After deducting the insurance payments of 10s 6d he would have a total of £11 7s 6d. His rent, if he is a council house tenant, plus rates and water charge, would be in the region of £1 8s 0d, and his expenditure on gas, light, and coal would amount to about £1 5s 0d per week. He is thus left with £8 14s 6d per week to feed and clothe a family of ten persons, not to mention other incidentals.

Within the framework of the present investigation it has not been possible to make a careful study of family budgets. The topic was discussed with the parents in the interview I had with them, but such information is of doubtful objective value. Some of the material has been incorporated in Chapter VI. The impression gained was that even the steady worker was unable to keep out of debt. Rent arrears are a normal pattern, and details are given in Chapter V. There is no literature dealing with incomes and expenditure in large families in this country, but a survey recently carried out by Field and Neill (1957) on a new housing estate in Belfast shows that fourteen per cent of the sample families belonged to a group who lived below the human-needs level. The average size of the family ranged between 5.7 for the group just below the human-needs level to 7.8 persons for the group whose income fell short of £1 10s below this level. The conclusions drawn in this survey are summed up in the following way: 'It is difficult to avoid concluding that an unskilled wage earner . . . who lived in a post-war house at a distance from his work could barely attain the Human Needs standard unless (1) his family is very small, or (2) there is more than one wage earner in the family, or (3) he has regular overtime.'

Lady Wootton (1959) also mentions the plight of 'those working-class families in which the breadwinner does not earn exceptionally high wages, and in which there are several young children and no supplementary earners. Children's allowances notwithstanding, families in this position have a very hard struggle'. These people form, in Lady Wootton's words, the Army of the New Poor. When they have to struggle along unsupported by friends or relations, as is the case in most of the families of the research set, the continuous interruptions of work of the wage earner to give the wife a hand have a serious effect on the wage packet and make an already precarious situation even worse.

C. *Incomes of men with indifferent work records.*

The fourteen men in this group present their families with a twin set of problems: a low income, and continuous adjustments of the household budget to changes in income. All the men are unskilled labourers with the exception of the man recently employed by the Blind Institute as a brushmaker. While in work these men would bring home some £8 10s 0d to £9 if they work a full week. When out of work they would draw unemployment or sickness benefit, both paid at the same rate. These rates are £4 12s 6d per week for husband and wife, 17s 6d for the first child, and 9s 6d for each subsequent child. In addition family allowances are drawn. Since these payments are insufficient to cover even essential needs, an application is usually made to the National Assistance Board for supplementary assistance, since none of the research families have any savings to fall back on. The National Assistance Board rates, in 1961, are for husband and wife £4 10s 0d per week, children under five 17s 0d, between five and eleven £1, and between eleven and sixteen £1 4s 0d per week. Rent is added separately and in the case of an applicant who is a householder the local rent rule is to cover the full rent, if considered 'reasonable'. When the needs of a family are calculated the income received from unemployment, sickness, or any other social benefit are taken into account, as well as family allowances, and normally the difference between this and the National Assistance Board scale is then paid out to the applicant. Certain other sources of income are disregarded up to a total of £1 10s 0d per week.

Although the above rates can in no way be considered high

55

they are based on estimates of subsistence costs. In an article in *The Times* of March 14, 1957, it was stated that

'In order to avoid too frequent adjustments, it is customary not to raise assistance scales until subsistence costs . . . have risen some way above them, and then to fix new scales well above the index.' This point was reached at the end of 1957, and again in March, 1961, the two most recent dates at which new rates were introduced.

The adequacy of the scale in operation will be discussed later. There is, however, another regulation which needs considering in connection with low income earners. This concerns the adjustment of allowances in relation to the wages normally earned by the applicant. Paragraph 5 of the National Assistance (Determination of Needs) Regulation (1948) states:

'The need for assistance of an applicant . . . shall not, unless there are special circumstances, be determined at an amount which, when taken together with his net weekly earnings from any regular part-time occupation, would exceed the amount of his net weekly earnings if he were employed full-time in his normal occupation.'

This regulation introduces the principle of the 'wages stop', or 'discretionary deduction', as it is commonly referred to, in computing allowances for applicants. It means in practice that, after computation of the total allowances accruing to a family, the usual spending wage of the applicant is taken into consideration and allowances are adjusted to be a few shillings below this. In cases of 'serious hardship' this regulation may be waived. The intention of the regulation is obvious: a man in receipt of assistance payments is not to be better off than if he were in work. If he is out of work he has no fares to work, no meals out, no wear and tear on clothes, and it is therefore considered reasonable that the total amount paid by the Assistance Board should be some five to ten shillings below his normal spending wage.

Two hypothetical examples of families will show that the effects of this regulation are more severe in the case of a large family. The state at which a discretionary deduction begins to be made depends on the number and ages of the children as well as on the previous income of the father. Assume that family A had three children aged four, eight, and twelve, and that the father is a labourer in a factory who normally earns £8 10s od.

After deduction of insurance his normal spending wage would be about £8 plus 18s od family allowances. While unemployed he applies for assistance allowances to make up his unemployment benefits and family allowances: The National Assistance Board would grant him the full allowance of £7 11s od plus full rent payment. This is probably less than his previous spending income of £8 18s od. Assume family B, on the other hand, to have eight children aged three, four, six, eight, ten, twelve, fourteen, fifteen. The father is an unskilled factory labourer whose weekly pay packet, after deduction of insurance contributions, is about eight pounds. His eight children entitle him to £3 8s od in family allowances, so that his total spendable income is £11 8s od per week. While unemployed the Assistance Board's allowances entitle him to £12 16s od plus rent. Since this is considerably higher than his normal spending money, a discretionary deduction of at least two pounds per week would be made; the exact figure depends on the size of rent. As the Assistance Board allowances are taken to be the minimum necessary for the maintenance of a subsistence level of living, the family B has an income below subsistence all the time, whether the father is in or out of work. The dilemma of the National Assistance Board is an obvious one, and the solution is obvious. The shortcomings uncovered through this regulation lie with the inadequacy of present family allowances.

The picture that emerges for the group of men in the survey who have indifferent work records is the following. When in work and working a full week their wages average between £8 10s od and £9 per week; when out of work their state-maintained incomes are somewhat less than their normal wages if they have a small family, and will be kept a few shillings below their normal spending wage by discretionary deductions in those cases where there are about six or more children to support. The level at which this rule operates depends, as mentioned before, on income, number and ages of children, and rent. Generally speaking, most of the men in the research set would be better off on assistance allowances than while at work if the system of discretionary deductions did not operate, as the average number of children in the research set is nearly seven. As it is, most of the men, whether in or out of work, have to manage on an income that is below the scale adopted by the Assistance

Board as the minimum necessary for the maintenance of a sub-sistence level of living.

D. Incomes of men with bad work records

There are twenty men with bad work records. These men are either disabled or suffer from chronic ill-health, physical or mental. Most of them have not had any employment for a con-siderable period and have exhausted their unemployment bene-fits. They are, therefore, entirely dependent on National Assist-ance Board payments and any disability pensions they may have. In two cases the wives have in recent years done some part-time work as cleaners or in factories. In both cases there are no children under school age. In a third family the wife has occasionally done part-time work. The first one pound net of any such earnings is disregarded in the computation of allow-ances. Discretionary deductions are made in the same way as has been described above.

National Assistance Board allowances are based on estimates of expenses covering minimum needs. In the above mentioned articles in The Times of March 14, 1957, these benefits are described as distinctly low in comparison with other advanced nations. But the article goes on to say that 'they are still above danger level, especially (thanks to enlarged family allowances) for the larger family'. This latter point may be true as long as the rule of discretionary deductions from allowances does not operate. Whether the scale of allowances can be considered to be 'above danger level' is another question. The scale is based on estimates of what is necessary for a minimum standard of living, and the items which are included in such estimates are of necessity arbitrary. Townsend (1955), in pointing out the arbitrary nature of such estimates, asks why—if clothing, fares to work, and newspapers are considered 'necessary'—such things as handkerchiefs, contraceptives, shaving and life insurance pay-ments are not included. He also raises the point whether it is right to use average expenditure of those who spend least as a basis upon which to calculate what people really need to spend to be out of poverty. Another approach in estimating minimum incomes is that of the food expert who presents a diet sheet necessary for the upkeep of health; the weekly requirements of the average working-class family are worked out at prevailing prices. The Bulletin of the Oxford University Institute of Statistics presents such a diet sheet twice a year. In one of the accompanying articles Schulz (1954) says:

'A "human needs" dietary must provide a selection of inexpensive foods that people will normally eat and it must provide for a nutritional intake that, at the time to which the specific dietary applies, is considered satisfactory; but subject to these qualifications the composition of the dietary is highly elastic. The changing pattern of our dietaries assumes indeed that a housewife is capable of adjusting her menus so as to profit by changes in supply and prices as circumstances permit.'

What weekly menu does Miss Schulz provide in her 'human needs' dietary? In the diet sheet for spring 1957 we find the following foods for a family consisting of father, mother, and three children: 4 lb. of meat, 1 lb. 8 oz. bacon, 8 oz. herrings, 12 eggs, 1 lb. 12 oz. cheese, 16 pts. milk, and 5 pts. free school milk, 2 tins condensed skimmed milk, 2 lb. 4 oz. margarine, 12 oz. dripping, 19 lb. 4 oz. bread, 3 lb. flour, 2 lb. 8 oz. rolled oats, 1 lb. 2 oz. other cereal, 2 lb. 8 oz. dried legumes, 21 lb. potatoes, 11 lb. fresh vegetables, 3 lb. sugar, 8 oz. tea, 4 oz. cocoa, 4 oz. syrup or jam, 8 oz. dried fruit. The total outlay at prevailing prices at that time was £3 9s 9d. There cannot be any doubt that this diet would keep a family of parents and three children in a reasonably fit state of health, but can it be maintained that such a selection of foods will provide stimulating and appetizing menus for a family with children in the long run? It may be noted that there is no provision for fresh fruit, or for tinned fruit, and there is only half a pound of dried fruit per week for a family of five. Only a quarter of a pound of syrup or jam is provided. The allocation of three pounds of sugar will not be sufficient for the provision of a pudding as well as the baking of cakes if all members of the family are used to sweetening their tea and their breakfast cereal.

But beyond this, are the assumptions that underlie the presentation of such a diet sheet for the use of the ordinary working-class housewife realistic? It is assumed, as prices change, that the housewife makes changes to minimize the increase in expenditure. A comparison of Miss Schulz's diet sheet of autumn 1954 with that of spring 1957 shows the following changes: In 1957 half a pound of bacon less was taken, and a half pound of sausages which had appeared on the 1954 sheet was omitted. Instead of one and a half pounds of herrings only half a pound was taken. This loss of protein was to be made up by two extra ounces of cheese per week (which had become cheaper), and by twelve eggs instead of three. One was also allowed an extra tin of skimmed milk, and an extra half a pound of dried legumes. On the other hand, one had to cut down the consumption of cereals by two ounces per week, and the consumption of sugar by a quarter pound. Such suggestions can really only be followed out if (i) the housewife has an excellent knowledge of proteins, carbohydrates, fats, vitamins, and the calorific values of available foods, and the requirements of these by the various members of the family, (ii) she is always fully informed of the prevailing prices and any changes, so as to be able to substitute one food by another of similar food value according to their relative prices, (iii) she has sufficient time to examine foods in various shops, and that she is within reach of cheap shops, and (iv) last but not least, none of her family have any particular fancies or dislikes, and all are equally willing to eat any food as long as it is the cheapest and contains the necessary food values for the preservation of life. It seems highly unrealistic to expect any of the above assumptions to operate when a working-class housewife, or for that matter, any housewife, is catering for her family. The total outlay of the size suggested by Miss Schulz appears to be a gross underestimate of what is actually spent. A more realistic approach would be the examination of actual working-class budgets and a comparison of these with the nutritional standards required for healthy living, as has been suggested by Townsend (1955).

It is, however, on the basis of some such expenditure that the families dependent on National Assistance allowances have to exist. Lady Wootton, in her book on Social Science and Social Pathology, points out that the population which is dependent on these allowances has constantly dropped below Seebohm Rowntree's poverty line in recent years, and it is only when NAB rates are raised to match increasing prices that allowances catch up with the minimum laid down by Rowntree (1951), and even that is not always achieved.

In Bristol an investigation was made into the budgeting of families who have lived on state-maintained incomes for more than one year. In an article describing the findings Shaw (1958) states: 'Most of the families found it so difficult as to be nearly impossible to live within income on statutory allowances when the interruption to earnings has lasted for more than twelve months . . . By that time any margin there might have been is used up, and it becomes impossible to replace or even repair anything that wears out. There seemed to be a process of cumulative deprivation, a progressive reduction of standards to the barest minimum of existence among those families who did manage to keep more or less within income. Our impression is that this can only be done by the exercise of considerable intelligence, rigorous self-discipline, and very skilful management of resources—a much greater task than the majority of us are called upon to face.' If this is the position facing ordinary families, how much more difficult must it be in families with large numbers of children, where wear and tear of clothes and equipment is much greater, and where, in addition, discretionary deductions are made from the ordinary allowances to bring the income into step with the previous working income. The National Assistance Board is empowered, in addition to paying allowances, occasionally to make special grants for the purchase of necessary articles or other unavoidable expenditure (National Assistance Determination of Needs Regulation, 1948, paragraph 6). A number of such 'exceptional needs grants' were made to some of the families in the research group during the five-year period. Some families were assisted in house-moving, others had grants for children's clothing and household goods. Several families never had any grants. It was not possible to find out whether they had applied for them.

To sum up, the twenty men with bad work records who have been living for long periods on National Assistance Board allowances to which discretionary deductions have been applied, have had to manage on incomes below subsistence level. For those with a large family the deduction has been considerable; for the three families with less than five children there was no deduction. For all the length of time on assistance has been a severe material strain.

3. CONCLUSIONS

This chapter has been concerned with an assessment of the material position of the fifty-two families. Certain patterns have emerged of adverse conditions which are bound to leave a mark on those who have to face them. The men with good work records have to carry the burden of either very large families whom they have to bring up on low incomes, or wives who are suffering from some disabilities. Often the two were combined. The men with bad work records, on the other hand, all suffer from some disability themselves, and in a number of cases—in fact half—the wives, too, are disabled. Most of the men in the group with indifferent work records are also physically or mentally handicapped, and only three enjoy normal health. None of the men in the survey are endowed with special abilities; the great majority are of the type that can expect only the lowest-paid kind of work. The sizes of the families is over three times the national average, and the income per head much below the average. (Average weekly earnings for men in all manufacturing industries in April, 1961, were £15 15s 3d for an average week of 47.3 hours (Ministry of Labour Gazette, August, 1961. HMSO). Indeed, it has been shown that, in the majority of cases where there are more than five children, the income is below subsistence level.

It is unfortunate that in the literature dealing with families who are suspected of child-neglect these extreme stress situations are rarely discussed, and emphasis is put instead on the parents' inability to make a success of their lives. This inability is frequently interpreted as an immaturity of personality, as for instance by Irvine (1954), Rankin (1958), and Bodman (1958). Ratcliffe (1958) traces this character trait back to a childhood of much insecurity which, he argues, can only be dealt with by some form of relationship therapy. While this diagnosis may be a correct one in many cases, it is obvious that it does not give a complete explanation. The conditions described above are bound to produce a considerable amount of anxiety and strain, and as the economic problems presented to these families appear to be insoluble they generate continuous frustration. Case-work therapy, however valuable otherwise, cannot be successfully applied in situations which fall short of what is considered essential. If our society demands the good life for all, based on subsistence income plus opportunity for individual initiative, it cannot at the same time ask its social therapists to acquaint some members of our society with the fact that they will not have the essentials and that they must adjust their personalities to it. Towle (1955), in an exposition of basic social-work concepts, stresses the importance of measures to relieve the sources of economic pressure and of strain, and she maintains that the economic burden carried by an adult should be 'commensurate with his capacity'. It appears that our society expects those with the lowest capacity to carry the heaviest economic burdens.

CHAPTER IV

THE CHILDREN

THERE are 386 children in the fifty-two families. They were not all living with their parents during the period of the survey; some were away in approved schools and in Children's Homes, although their parents were still legal guardians. Twenty-five children had left home for good; fourteen were in the care of the local authority, two had been adopted by other people, seven were living with a parent from a former marriage, and two boys had emigrated to Australia. Of the remaining children 190 were boys, and 171 girls. There were, in December, 1955, 86 children under school age, 193 children at school, and 82 adolescents.

Four sources provided the information contained in this chapter: the school teachers, the welfare office of the education department, the health visitors, and, when applicable, the child guidance clinic. The parents, too, provided a good deal of background colouring, but the opinions expressed by them on education and other matters affecting their children have been incorporated into Chapter VI. The teachers assessed educational attainments, conduct and appearance at school. The school welfare office made available attendance sheets for two terms for each of the school children, and supplied information concerning educational prosecutions. The health visitors talked about the children's physique and health. The child guidance clinic supplied intelligence quotients of those children who had sat a test, and gave more detailed information in the few cases which had been referred to the clinic for treatment.

1. PHYSIQUE AND HEALTH

Under the National Health Act the health visitor of a local authority has a statutory obligation to visit each new-born baby, and after satisfying herself that the baby is progressing normally she will continue to visit at least twice annually until the child is of school age. Once it is at school, the child will be seen by the school nurse at regular intervals. The health visitors of the areas in which the research families live were, therefore, able to give information concerning at least the more serious physical deviations or illnesses that the children had. There were ten children who had some physical abnormality like deformed hip, deformed hand, or defective feet requiring orthopaedic footwear. Nine children had squints, and three suffered from deafness. There were five children who suffered from skin trouble of the asthma-eczema group, six had stammers or other speech defects, one was epileptic, and one had a nervous breakdown in adolescence. Ten children had tuberculosis, one suffered from severe anaemia, and one had unspecified gland trouble. Many of the otherwise normal children were described as thin, pale, undernourished or undersized.

2. INTELLIGENCE

At the time the survey was carried out, 193 children were at school. There were 51 in infant schools, 76 in junior schools, 47 in secondary schools, one in a technical school, and one in a grammar school. Two children were in an occupation centre, and fifteen in residential schools.

The children in the infant schools sit a group intelligence test (Moray House Pictorial Test) before entering the junior school. They sit a further group test (Moray House 11-plus test) before entering the secondary school. The children under seven had not undergone any testing, and the only obtainable information about their intelligence was an assessment by their teachers. It is difficult, however, in making such assessments to distinguish mental ability from educational attainments, and attainments are bound to suffer from irregular school attendance, a matter which is more fully discussed below. Of the seventy-six children in junior schools the results of the Moray House Pictorial Test were available for forty-eight, and of the forty-nine children in secondary schools the results for thirty-five were available. The reasons for the large number of unobtainable IQs are that twenty children were not presented for the tests because they were believed to have no chance of scoring well, that in addition it was difficult to get information from the voluntary schools,

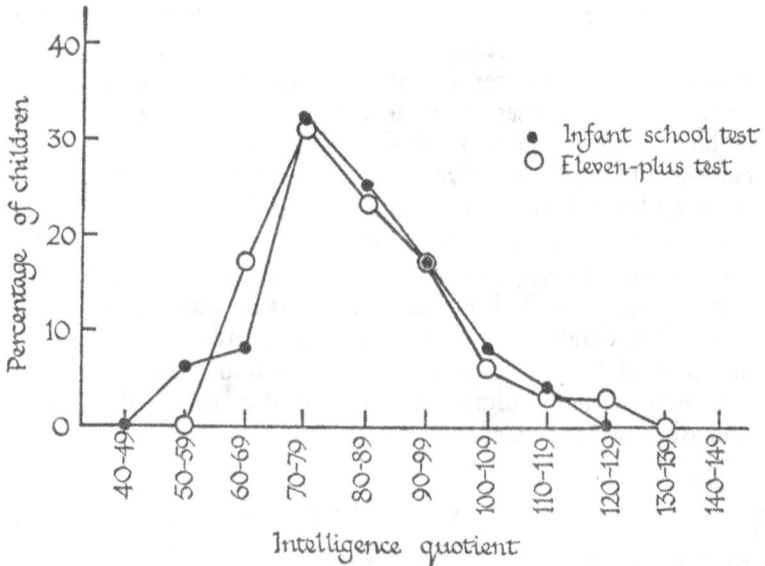

Fig. 1. Distribution curve of intelligence quotients of research-family children.

and that in a few isolated cases the information was not available for administrative reasons.

Although group tests have very severe limitations they do offer a rough yardstick for measurement of intelligence, and are preferable to any subjective assessment. The results obtained for the seven-year-old children are based on a pictorial test which is not as precise as the test applied in the 11-plus examination. The average intelligence quotients obtained for the two groups are, however, surprisingly similar: 82.5 for the seven-year-olds, and 81.4 for the eleven-year-olds. (The curve of the distribution of the IQs is given in Fig. 1, p. 66.) By far the majority of both groups have IQs between seventy and ninety. If to these are added the twenty children who were not presented to sit the tests because of their expected low performance, it can be regarded as certain that the curve of distribution of IQs is displaced widely to the lower end of the scale.

The low average IQ of around eighty-two must be interpreted

at least partially as artificially depressed by environmental conditions. Very poor living conditions, absence of cultural stimuli in the home, overcrowding, and irregular school attendance are known to have an adverse effect on the development of intelligence. Jones (1946) in discussing this also stresses the importance of personal non-ability factors which, if traumatic, may affect mental growth directly. There may be, in addition, another factor in the families under investigation, and that is the large family. Nisbet (1953), in an investigation of family environment and intelligence, shows that there is a negative correlation between family size and intelligence, and he argues that this may be connected with the verbal development of the young child. A survey carried out by the Scottish Council for Research in Education (quoted by Woodward, 1955) has shown that this correlation holds good within every occupational class, and that the combination of overcrowding and large families was associated with the lowest scores. But beyond these environmental influences there is the the fact of hereditary potentiality: adverse circumstances cannot altogether stunt a brilliant brain, nor can the most advantageous environment develop a poorly endowed one.

The children in the survey all have manual labourers for their fathers; some are skilled, most are unskilled. Tests have shown that the average IQs obtained by pre-school children arranged in groups classified by their fathers' occupations drop by something like twenty points from the professional to the unskilled. The mean IQs quoted by Jones (1946) are arranged in the following order:

Occupation of father	Mean IQ of children
Professional	116
Semi-professional and managerial	112
Clerical and skilled trades	108
Semi-skilled and minor clerical	104
Slightly skilled	95
Unskilled	94

It could be expected, therefore, that the children of the research set of families would have a mean IQ of about ninety-four, the average for children of unskilled labourers. It is in fact considerably below this figure. The mean IQ, however, does not demonstrate the width of range, and, as has been pointed out by Vernon (1957), there is a good deal of overlapping between occupational groups. It appears that the children in the survey belong to the group who make up the lower half of the curve for unskilled labourers.

3. EDUCATIONAL ATTAINMENTS

Progress at school is closely linked to mental ability as well as to attendance at school. Other factors, such as physical well-being and emotional conditions also influence the process of learning. Is the child ready to learn if he has just witnessed a quarrel between his parents? Or he might have come to school with no breakfast; Mother was not up in time, or there was nothing to eat in the house. He might be wearing shoes that are too small and that have blistered his feet; or he might be sore because he still wets and his clothes have not been changed. The assessments that the teachers made of the children's educational attainments must be judged in the light of such knowledge.

These assessments were categorized in the following way. In the first place, the number of 'streams' into which a class had been divided was ascertained. Secondly, the teachers were asked to assess the child's position in the stream as 'above average', 'average', or 'below average'. If the class consisted of two or more streams, the teachers' assessment was adjusted according to the stream the child belonged to. For instance, a child in the lowest of four streams, but assessed as above average for the stream was classified as below average. A child in the upper stream of two, but below average for the stream, was classified as average. All children attending special schools for educationally subnormal children were grouped as below average, even though some might be doing well in the special school.

Assessments were available for 167 children. Of these the great majority, 122, were assessed as below average in educational attainments; thirteen of them were attending special schools. Thirty-five children were assessed as average, and ten as above average. Three of these ten children have sat the eleven-plus examination; one obtained a place in a grammar school, another a place in a secondary technical school, but the third with a good IQ has not managed to get a grammar school place.

4. SCHOOL ATTENDANCE

The question arises whether low educational attainment is not only linked with poor mental endowment, but is artifically depressed by bad school attendance. Did the good attenders on the whole perform better than the bad attenders within a given IQ group? If that could be shown to be true, it would indicate that the children did not suffer unduly from emotional upsets, but reacted like ordinary emotionally well-adjusted children. Furthermore, although the average IQ in the group was much below normal, there were a number of children of normal and some of above normal intelligence; did they make full use of their ability, or did bad attendance depress their attainments? Lastly,

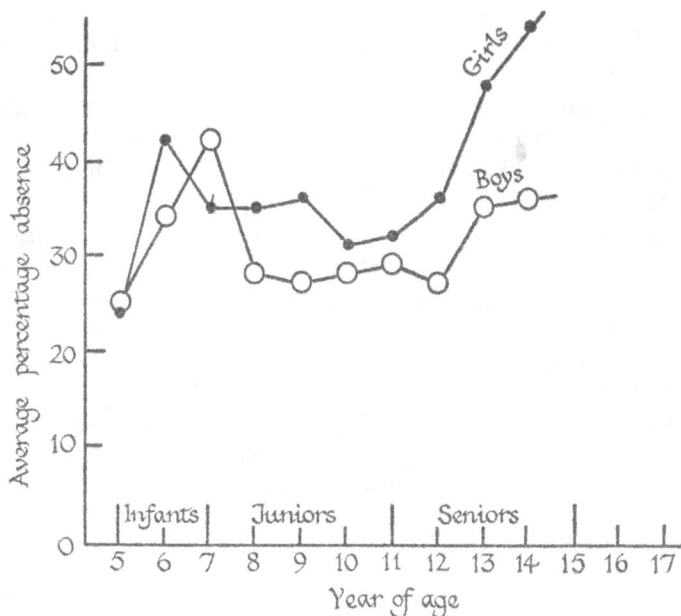

Fig. 2. Average percentage absence over two terms of the bad attenders. The 36 good attenders are not included.

who were the bad attenders? Were there certain families who did not bother to send their children? Or was it mainly the eldest children in each family who were kept home for chores? Or was bad attendance confined to adolescents?

School attendance was measured by ascertaining the total number of morning and afternoon periods that a child was absent from school over two terms and dividing this by the total possible attendances. In a very few cases where a child was new at school, only one term's attendance could be worked out. If no full term's records were available, that child was not rated. Records were thus available for 164 children. In establishing a norm of what might be considered satisfactory attendance we have lowered the percentage of expected attendances accepted as normal in the local education department. Ninety-five per cent attendance is locally considered normal; to allow for periods of genuine illness we lowered the norm to 90 per cent. All children whose absences did not exceed 10 per cent during two terms have been classified as normal attenders.

It was at once apparent that school attendance is not taken very seriously among the research families. Some families, however, did rather worse than others; but only 22 per cent of the children were normal attenders. A quarter of the children had absences of 40 per cent and over. These absences were not confined to adolescents, although the teenagers did rather worse than the younger children; there was also a distinct rise in absences for both boys and girls during the last term at infant school. The junior school has on the whole the best attendances, and one wonders whether the competition for the eleven-plus test has anything to do with this. (A curve of percentage absences as a function of age appears in fig. 2, p. 69.)

No such clear pattern was discernible when the percentage absence of the eldest child in the family was compared to the rate of absence of his or her younger sibs. Among the boys there were twelve who had a worse attendance record than their younger sibs, and there were another seven who did rather better than the younger ones in the family. Among the girls the picture was equally confused; thirteen eldest girls missed more school than the rest of their families, and nine girls were better attenders than the other children in their families. It was obvious that the often-repeated story, mother keeps the eldest home to help, is a myth. The slightly greater preponderance of absences of eldest children is probably sufficiently accounted for by the tendency for absences to increase with age throughout the secondary school.

Bad school attendance means either neglect on the part of the parents or deliberate non-attendance, or truancy, on the part of the child. In fact the picture that emerged made it very difficult to distinguish between the two. In many cases the parents were taken to court and were fined for failure to send a particular child to school. In many other cases children were put under the supervision of a probation officer because they failed to attend. A clear distinction between parental and filial responsibility seems hardly possible. The Education (Miscellaneous Provisions) Act, 1953, under section 11 enables a local authority to bring a persistently truant child directly before the juvenile court as an alternative to, as well as in addition to, bringing the parents before an adult court. Of the fifty-two families two had children only under school age; of the rest twenty-eight families had been to court, some only once, some more often. One family had paid seventeen fines for non-attendance of their several children. Seven of these families had additional supervision orders, and there was also one supervision order in one family who had not had any educational prosecutions. The usual procedure is to make enquiries if a child is absent for two weeks or longer without a medical certificate. If the period exceeds one month, a 'final notice' is sent before the case goes to court. The fines paid by the parents range between 10s and £5. The parents who had no educational prosecutions are almost all parents with younger children, whose combined number of school years are considerably less than those of the prosecuted families. This suggests that the difference in school attendance records is not primarily one of attitudes, but rather one of age composition.

How does absence from school affect the educational attainments of those children whose IQs are around 100? It is obvious that the child who does not attend regularly is bound to fall behind; whether such a child would substantially improve his position in class by better attendance depends very much on his readiness to learn. There were thirteen children whose IQs ranged between 96 and 116. Four of them had been assessed as above average by their teachers; three as average; and the remaining six as below average. On working out the attendance records of this group, it was at once apparent that there was a correlation between absence and educational attainments. The four children who did well at school were all normal attenders; the highest percentage absence was eleven. Their IQs ranged between 115—100. The six who did badly, had IQs between 116 and 96, and their rates of absence were between 15 per cent and 44 per cent. There was one exception, a girl whose recent rate of absence was only 8 per cent; this was the result of an educational prosecution, she had been a very bad attender before. The middle group, who were assessed as average by their teachers had IQs between 103 and 100 and their rates of absence were between 6 and 12 per cent. It appears that all these children performed as would be expected of a normal child with no particular maladjustments.

As a further test of the validity of this observation we asked whether all good attenders who nevertheless were assessed as below average in educational attainments were of low intelligence. There were sixteen children who were 'normal' attenders (i.e. absences did not exceed 10 per cent) with educational attainments below average. Six of them attended voluntary schools and their IQs could not be ascertained. Two children were not presented for the eleven-plus tests as they were considered unable to pass it. Seven children had IQs between fifty-eight and ninety-two. There was another girl from the above-mentioned family in this group who had only recently improved her school attendance record. She had an IQ of ninety-nine and could obviously have done better if she had not had a bad record of absences before her parents were taken to court. Here again a close correlation between attendance and attainments was observable.

The picture we obtained in linking intelligence, educational attainments and school attendance may be summed up in the following way:

(i) The average intelligence of the group is well below the national average, and even below the average quoted for unskilled labourers' children. The mean infant-test IQ is just over eighty-two, and the mean eleven-plus IQ is just over 81.

(ii) About three-quarters of the children are below average in educational attainments, and only 7 per cent are above average within their age groups.

(iii) About 80 per cent of the children are bad school attenders; the average percentage of absence over two terms is thirty-six.

(iv) Bad attendance is in evidence even during the first year at the infant school. Over the whole period at the infant school only about a quarter of the children are good attenders, and the others have an average rate of absence of over 34 per cent.

(v) By the time the children have reached the ages of thirteen or fourteen, the percentage of good attenders drops to fifteen, and the rate of absence of the others rises to over 43 per cent.

(vi) There is a close correlation between IQ, attendance and educational attainments, which suggests that there is little maladjustment.

5. BEHAVIOUR

The information collected under this heading is necessarily of a subjective nature. Unlike other assessments made in this survey concerning parental abilities and relationships in the family, which were made by two workers, the children's conduct could be ascertained from one source only, the teachers in charge of the child at the time of the investigation. It was therefore not considered necessary to standardize questions and answers. The wide range of spontaneous observations made by the teachers proved to be a rich source of information about his relationship with the child, from which it appeared that on the whole these children are no great problem to their teachers. There were 143 behavioural assessments; in a number of cases the teachers said they were unable to say anything about the child because the child attended too rarely. In only twenty-seven cases (seventeen boys and ten girls) did the teachers feel that the children were a problem, that their behaviour was undisciplined, that they were completely out of hand, bad, resentful, or aggressive. In ninety-two cases the children were described as fundamentally nice, sociable, good-natured, normal, no trouble, or at least 'fair'. There was, in addition, a group of twenty-four children (nine boys and fifteen girls) who were described as very quiet, negative, shy, craving attention or affection, unpopular; and to this was usually added some comment about the children's deprivations.

The teachers also commented on the children's appearance, their cleanliness, the state of their clothes, and whether or not the mothers co-operated when asked to do so. Clothes and cleanliness were almost invariably commented on as 'shocking' even in schools where there were many children from low-income homes. Comments such as the following were frequent: Badly clothed, inadequately clothed, queerly dressed, e.g. boy wearing women's shoes, or shoes borrowed from sib, too large or too small, or wearing father's shirt or jacket; cotton frocks in mid-winter; wearing the same dress all the time, never washed; no handkerchiefs; Wellingtons in hot weather; needs haircut; smells. Sometimes the teachers added that the mothers were trying their best under very difficult circumstances; in other cases they pointed out that the mothers were not co-operative and resented the teachers' 'interference'. One teacher told me that she had bathed and powdered a five-year-old who was not toilet-trained, and then sent her home with a note saying that her underwear must be changed more frequently. In consequence the mother kept the child at home for a fortnight, until the school welfare officer managed to persuade her to return to school. The problem of toilet-training was particularly commented on by infant teachers; the smell of soaked clothing was often mentioned as an explanation why other children shun these children.

Speech difficulties, particularly during the infant school stage, were frequently mentioned. The children appeared to be far behind the normal child in being able to express themselves. Infant school teachers frequently mentioned that they had to fetch elder brothers or sisters to interpret during some crisis. Quite obviously no adult had taken the trouble to talk to the child and correct his speech before he entered school. Sometimes 'bad language' and swearing was also mentioned. One of the major problems, however, appeared to be the absence of self-discipline in the child. At home the children did not get any training of any kind; consequently the demands made by the teacher for attentiveness, regularity, punctuality, and so on, were much more difficult to meet for a child of this home background than they are for a child from a normal home. The following comments were made by the Head Teacher of an infant school which is close to an area that houses a considerable number of problem families.

'Although not conscious of it, the children from problem families bring their home environment with them when they come to school. They react in school to the environment they know. This is sometimes a crisis for the child, especially when the two environments are so very different. Children from problem families are very conscious of this clash . . . One hears comments (from teachers) such as these: They show no response, their movements are clumsy, they find it difficult to use their hands, especially to handle small objects, e.g. pencils, crayons, small apparatus. They appear to be detached from the rest of the class.

'Children from problem families are usually of one of two types. A child may be found to be unruly, noisy, and anti-social towards other children, or more often appears quiet, uncommunicative, detached, unresponsive to overtures from children and teachers, and appears to retreat into himself and be overcome by the new environment. He can so easily become a trial to himself and the teacher unless she fully realizes that his failures to respond are due to his difficulty to adjust himself to so many new demands. His mistakes are so often made through ignorance.

'He so often shows a lack of care of everything. Clothes are thrown in the cloakroom and not hung on a hook. School apparatus is handled roughly and broken easily. It is thrown down and not placed in a cupboard where it can be found again. When an article is needed, it is snatched. There are no such words as "please" and "thank you". Sometimes it will take a child a long time before he will venture to use apparatus at all. Such children are not used to playing with toys at home. They will just look around overwhelmed with what is going on around them. They lack confidence, which makes it difficult to help them . . .

'These children appear backward when compared with their contemporaries. It may not really mean that they are less intelligent but that they need to be given more time. They start school with a handicap.

'The speech of children from problem families is usually very poor. Vocabulary is very poor and articulation bad. This is rarely the result of any special impediment in the speech but rather because no one has taken the trouble to help the child pronounce words properly. There is no fluency in conversation, speech is so often a jumble of words. It is sometimes amazing to find that these children will play together and understand one another perfectly while others cannot do so. The effect of speech difficulty results in backwardness in reading. Until speech improves a child makes little progress in reading. Slowness to show reading readiness is of course due to lack of books in the home. This is evident in the lack of interest at first shown in the classroom book corner . . . When finally an interest has been stimulated the care of the books is a constant worry to the teacher.

'It has been found that the children from problem families show a quicker response to number teaching than many other subjects. They show a surprising knowledge of money values. This is because at a very early age they are sent shopping for mother.

'Experience with children from problem families emphasizes the fact that the school must be prepared to take the responsibility to teach habits . . . Children do not mind being dirty and unkempt if they have no other standards. They have to be encouraged and helped continually as so often there appears to be hardly any help from home. Much can be done by a friendly approach to the mother but so often there are lapses caused by something in the home beyond the control of the school. This lack of cleanliness and untidiness has its effects on all the child's school possessions. Replacements of broken and untidy books need to be constantly made . . . When school meals are taken it is noticeable that so much of the food given is strange; bread, meat and potatoes they are familiar with but they need to be constantly encouraged to eat greens, carrots, swedes, and salads. Spoons and hands are used more often than knives and forks.

'Attendance at school of children from problem families is poor. It appears worse in winter than summer. Lack of clothing and footwear is definitely a cause sometimes. It can also be failure of the mother to rise in time, or no food in the house for breakfast. Occasionally the cause is because some article of clothing cannot be found although taken off the previous night . . . Some clothing is shared by children in a family. Parents take a careless attitude towards school attendance. Children are kept home to care for younger ones, to run messages and just to fetch and carry.

'Constant absences from school have a very detrimental effect on children's progress at school. Even when a child shows signs of ability, constant absences cannot be overcome. The child becomes conscious that he is behind in his work and gradually loses heart and interest in his own progress and achievement.

'During physical education lessons the child finds it difficult to take his proper place in the class because of ill-fitting clothes and footwear. Boys feel this more than girls. Their shoes are often clumsy, trousers are badly fastened, the child is uncomfortable, shoes are difficult to remove and difficult to replace after the lesson. Removal of some clothing during the lesson is an embarrassment for the older children especially when it reveals dirty feet and legs. No child can be expected to enjoy this lesson unless he is comfortably clothed.

'Confusion about possessions is sometimes a difficulty. There is confusion about articles of clothing missing from the cloakroom. Mistakes are often made because children find difficulty in recognizing their own things. Rarely is an article of outdoor clothing bought for the child. He wears someone else's cast-offs or clothes bought at a jumble sale. How can he recognize something he is not quite sure of? There is no real pride in it. It is a case of 'any old thing can be mine'.

'However poor the home, the children seem to be fond of it. They appear loyal to their parents and see no fault in them. It is probably because they know no other standard with which to make comparisons. It is not until the children are much older that criticism becomes evident.'

6. LEISURE-TIME ACTIVITIES

To round off the picture it should be mentioned that none of the school children of the research set were members of any youth clubs or organizations such as Boy Scouts or Girl Guides. This information was obtained in the course of the interview with the mother or father. The adolescents could not be interviewed individually, and the parents often stated that the children were out at night frequently, and that they could not tell where they were or what they were doing.

7. EMPLOYMENT OF THE ADOLESCENTS

What kind of employment and what quality of life can be expected of the young men and women who grew up in the families described in these pages? Their younger brothers and sisters appear to be predominantly of a poorly endowed type, they attend badly at school, and their performance in school suffers in consequence. Some of the special handicaps, such as inadequate clothing, a neglected appearance, and poor speech, would suggest that these children grow up ill-prepared for a life of economic independence. Certain factors that may affect their character development will be discussed in Chapter VIII. The present observations are merely factual, and are based on the obtainable employment records of adolescent boys and girls in the survey. The information was obtained primarily from the Youth Employment Bureau and, in some cases, from the Criminal Records Department. In a few cases the only informant was the parent.

There are thirty-seven boys above school age, with ages ranging up to twenty-seven. The three oldest (ages twenty-seven, twenty-six and twenty-five) are married and away from home. No information was obtained about them. One young man, aged twenty-four, is in the Navy, and one, aged twenty, served an apprenticeship in a racing stable away from home, and is now working as a jockey. None of the others over twenty have had any special training, or have remained in one type of employment since leaving school. There are six, and brief accounts of their records follow. The names are fictitious.

Leonard, aged 25. Long record of quick changes, unemployed for lengthy periods, sometimes not drawing benefit, interspersed with Borstal and prison sentences. Has had jobs as builder's labourer, casual dock labourer, in a circus, and in factories.

Nelson, aged 24. Labourer in factories, laundry, building sites, dairy, coal merchant. Called up, discharged from army after a few weeks. Directed to mines, left after medical examination as unfit. Coal merchant, brick works, trawler, mill hand, building sites, bakery, ironmonger, brewery, interspersed with Borstal and prison. Married, two children.

Charles, brother of Nelson, aged 22. Brickworks, dairy, builders, garage, unemployed, not drawing benefit. At present serving prison sentence.

Donald, aged 21. British Railways, cinema, two years army, garage, British Railways. Married, one child.

Martin, aged 21. Laundry, unemployed, Corporation labourer, builder's labourer.

Steven, brother of Martin, aged 20. Released from approved school at age 17, Corporation labourer, van boy.

Albert, aged 20. Released from approved school at age 17, various labourer's jobs, lasting short periods. Army. At present unemployed.

The remaining twenty-seven are under twenty years of age, and have varying records. Since most of them (twenty in fact) are seventeen or younger it cannot be assumed with certainty that none of them will ever develop regular work habits. All that can be said is that there is a great deal of changing of jobs which cannot be entirely explained by the normal restlessness experienced by young men who are waiting to be called up. In a report published by the Council of King George's Jubilee Trust (1955) it was stated that the Youth Employment Service had found that slightly less than half of the boys aged 15-18 stayed in their first jobs, and about one in three had changed their jobs once. The remaining one in six had changed their jobs twice or more. The pattern of continuous change found in the research set of adolescents appears to be a deviation from the normal.

There are forty-five girls above school-leaving age. Eleven are married and live away from their parents. No information was obtained about them. There are another five over the age of twenty, and brief records of their careers follow. The names are fictitious.

Jane, aged 27. Café waitress in various places, cinema. Then lived on prostitution. Has a number of convictions. At present a TB hospital in-patient.

Margaret, sister of Jane, aged 22. Shop assistant, factory work, cinema usherette, café waitress. Then lived mainly on prostitution, several convictions. At present TB hospital in-patient.

Virginia, aged 22. Steady record as a café waitress.

Pamela, sister of Virginia, aged 21. Factory, cinema usherette, domestic help, café waitress. Each job lasting from three to five months.

Mary, aged 20, sister of Nelson and Charles. Is considered 'nervous' by her parents, lives at home, unemployed.

There are twenty-nine girls under twenty, none of them married. The job preference for the under-twenties seems to be factory work or laundry work. As with the boys, there is a tendency to frequent changes. Jane and Margaret, quoted above, are the only girls to become professional prostitutes.

As will be discussed in Chapter VII, there is a high rate of juvenile delinquency among these young people. This is bound to have a bearing on their employment records.

CHAPTER V

HOUSING CONDITIONS

SEAPORT has an estimated population of about a quarter million people. The town developed very rapidly after the opening of the docks in the mid-nineteenth century. It became an important centre for the export of coal, but in recent years this trade has declined considerably. Seaport is now increasingly becoming the centre for many administrative services.

The oldest districts are those near the docks, and some of them have been scheduled for slum clearance. The local authority owns a group of houses in this area, but the greater part of the municipal property is to be found on the outlying housing estates. Most of the research families are council tenants, and only fourteen live in privately-owned rented accommodation. It cannot be concluded, however, that this is a true sample of all such families in Seaport, as the original referral to the Co-ordination Committee depended on the discretion of the various referral agents. Furthermore, the fact that none of the fifty-two families were living in rooms during the investigation must not be taken as significant. A number of the initial 157 families were in rooms, but had moved to unknown addresses before they could be interviewed. Because these families move more frequently it is likely that they do not come to the notice of the local authority as easily as tenants of a council house.

Of the fifty-two families in the research set, seven had gone into a council house straight from a squatters' camp, and four from the local authority's welfare accommodation for homeless mothers and children. Most of the others had been living in rooms or with their parents, and had, because of their large numbers of children, qualified for council houses. The housing department applies a grading system and, if general standards are low, the applicants are normally offered old property. It is primarily for this reason that there is an accumulation of the families in two areas, in which there are the oldest council houses dating back to 1922-1923. One of these districts is close to the docks, the other on an outlying housing estate. A few families live in comparative isolation from one another in slightly newer council houses, and two have recently been moved to houses built after 1945 on the two newest estates. The fourteen families who are not council tenants are widely distributed over the older parts of the city.

Under what conditions do these families live? First of all, let us look at the problem of overcrowding. Real overcrowding cannot be demonstrated effectively by merely counting numbers of persons and numbers of rooms. There were many families in the survey who did not use all the accommodation in the house they occupied, because they did not have enough furniture. Beds are usually shared by parents and children, particularly during the colder months, because of the shortage of bedclothing. Living rooms in some houses were entirely unfurnished, and the family used the kitchen for their day-time activities. Real over-crowding in terms of the rooms actually used is therefore greater than can be expressed in terms of average density per room. But even the latter shows that the research families were considerably more overcrowded than other families living in their neighbourhoods. In the Docks' area the research families showed a density of 1.9 per room, whereas the average for the district is only 0.85. The research families living in Broomhill, the housing estate, had a density of 1.7 per room, as against an average density of 0.97. The families living in privately-owned accommodation which they rented had on the average one room to two persons. The average for the whole of Seaport is 0.77 per room. (1951 Census.)

The problem of rents and rent arrears is, of course, a different one for council tenant or private tenant. The council tenant in Seaport is subject to a rent-rebate scheme which was introduced in 1957 to supersede a differential-rent scheme. Under the new scheme the tenant may apply for a reduction of the basic rent fixed for his house, the maximum reduction being 11s od per week. Roughly, the rent chargeable to the tenant is calculated on the basis of one-eighth of his income, and an allowance of 1s 6d is made for each dependent child. If this amounts to a figure between the basic rent and 11s od less than the basic rent, it is the amount of rent paid. If it is more than the basic rent, the basic rent is paid. If it is less than the basic rent minus 11s od, the basic rent minus 11s od is paid. There are adjustments for earning children, earning wives, or lodgers. Since almost all the men in the research set were low-income earners with large families, it is to be expected that they would occupy three- or four-bedroom houses with the lowest basic rents. Basic rents are calculated according to the size of the house and its amenities, and consideration is given to the age of the house. The smaller houses in the 'docks' and the concrete houses in the outlying district referred to as 'Broomhill', which are the oldest council property, have the lowest basic rents. It is not surprising, therefore, that a number of the research families are to be found in these houses. This is not to say that such a concentration is necessarily recommendable from the social worker's point of view.

The rents paid by the thirty-eight tenants vary considerably. Not only does the range stretch from the fully rebated to the basic rent, but the rent paid by an individual tenant may fluctuate considerably with fluctuations in earnings. One man, for instance, when in work as a boiler scaler, earned an amount which, in addition to the earnings of his eldest children, did not qualify him for a rebate. When out of work, however, he qualified for it. In the last quarter of 1957 twelve research families paid the full rent, which varied from £1 7s 2d to £1 13s 10d per week, including rates and water charges. The twenty-six tenants who had a rebate during that period paid between 15s 8d and £1 8s 1d. The latter high rent is a fully rebated rent on a post-war house.

If the low income per head of most of the research families is taken into consideration, it is not surprising that most of them have arrears. This applies in particular to the men whose work records are choppy. When unemployed, the income is low and debts are usually incurred. When in work a higher rent may have to be paid, and that makes the repayment of debts more difficult. When there is a general shortage of money, the temptation is great to let the rent go unpaid for a week or so, since the consequences of such a step are not as immediate as they would be, for instance, with a grocer's debt. It takes a considerable time before the housing department obtains a possession order and evicts, or until it obtains a judgment summons on the strength of which a tenant may be committed to prison for non-payment of a court order.

In fact, the accumulation of rent arrears was very widespread during the period 1953-1957 when the old differential-rent scheme was in operation. Under this scheme a declaration of income during the preceding thirteen weeks had to be handed in; if this was not done the tenant was charged a maximum rent. If he refused to pay this, arrears would mount. There were no allowances for dependants. Sometimes statements were made which were not accurate, and when in 1956 wages declarations were obtained from employers to check tenants' incomes the arrears were back-dated by a year. An item in a local newspaper of February 25, 1956, stated: 'As a result of the tightening up of the differential rents scheme it has been discovered that 2,627 tenants who did not disclose their full income owe £42,302 in arrears. This report was given at a meeting of the Corporation Estates Committee on Wednesday by the Manager, Mr ——, who added, "We have not yet completed our investigation, but since April last arrears have gone up from £7,594 to £50,000". It was stated that some of the tenants have £40 arrears to make up, but arrangements were being made to pay instalments.'

It appears that this old differential-rent scheme brought about an arrears-sophistication which is now difficult to eradicate. Rent arrears were one of the few items concerning finances that were freely discussed with me in the interviews I had with the parents. The usual undertone was that 'they' put on some arrears for which the tenant could hardly be blamed, but which were entirely the result of a stupid scheme. Criticism of this scheme was heavy; it was considered particularly unfair to families with many children since it took no account of dependents in assessing rents. The scheme was abolished and replaced by the rebate scheme in April, 1957, but the arrears accumulated under the old scheme were entered into the new rent books. Some tenants were unwilling to pay these debts, and have in addition incurred further arrears. Consequently they have reached a size which is difficult to tackle; some of the research families had considerable arrears.

Only three out of the thirty-eight council tenants in the research set had never contracted any rent arrears; but their tenancies were only six years, two years, and one year respectively at the time of the survey. At that time four rents were being paid directly to the housing department by the National Assistance Board through a third party, and one by the employer, a Corporation department. There were seven tenants who had no arrears at the time, but who showed arrears in their rent books which they had managed to clear. There were another nine families who had long records of rent arrears not exceeding £15 at any one time; and nineteen families with a long record of arrears exceeding £15 at one time or another.

These families with large rent arrears have given the housing department a good deal of trouble. Arrears often accumulated within a year of moving into a council house. A 'notice to quit' would sometimes have the desired effect, but often it would be followed by a possession order. The court costs would then be added to the arrears and swell them still further. Sometimes the family would be transferred to a cheaper house and would then, for a time, be more regular in paying rent. Sometimes, however, there would be no improvements, and ejectment warrants would be executed. After a period in rooms and some of the children in the care of the Children's Officer, the family might later be offered another house. Although the differential-rent scheme had aggravated the problem, there is evidence that arrears were accumulated even before this scheme was introduced in 1953. While this scheme was in operation the size of arrears rose steeply.

It might be thought that the families with lowest incomes per head accumulated the largest debts, but this was not so. In fact, the existence of rent arrears could not be correlated to any index such as size of family, father's income, or his work record. It turned out that some of the socially most maladjusted men had a clear rent book, and conversely some of the families with large arrears belonged to the group of steady workers with normal health who showed no deviancy of behaviour. The three tenants with no rent arrears had the following records:

1. Tenant since 1950, after living at squatters' camp. Unemployed, probably now unemployable. History of mental instability. Convicted of assaults on young girls and other offences. Has six children.

2. Tenant for two years, previously in one furnished room.

Disabled, unemployed, with poor prospects. Several criminal convictions. Four children.

3. Tenant for one year, previously in two furnished rooms. Mother has five children from three fathers. Present head of family old-age pensioner.

The seven tenants who had managed to clear their arrears included five with long criminal records and very choppy work records, and one with a history of mental instability. These cases show that some people with anti-social character traits are 'satisfactory tenants' as seen from the viewpoint of a housing department's accounts office; whereas 'unsatisfactory tenants' may include reasonably stable people whose only problem is a low income per head. The realization of this may help to clear some of the confusion that exists at present in considering unsatisfactory tenants as being synonymous with families in need of social therapy.

The neighbourhoods in which the fifty-two families live vary considerably. As has been mentioned earlier, the housing department applies a grading scheme to the living conditions of applicants for council houses. If an applicant scores low he is likely to be offered one of the old types of houses, which were built in 1922-1923. In addition to their sub-standard quality ('It does not matter if they get knocked about') the basic rents for these houses are the lowest, and therefore can be best afforded by a low-income tenant. Of the thirty-eight council tenants in the research set twenty-six lived in such houses. Nine families lived in slightly newer and better inter-war houses on one of the estates, and two on post-war estates. One family lived in the centre of the town in a pre-war house now owned by the Corporation. The fourteen families in non-council houses will be discussed later.

There are, then, three distinct groups of families in council houses, leaving out for the time being the three families in relative isolation. There is (i) the group in terraced and semi-detached houses near the docks, (ii) the group in old houses on the Broomhill estate, and (iii) a slightly more scattered group in newer houses on the same estate.

(i) The houses in the docks area are of varying types. The smaller terraced type has two bedrooms, and one room downstairs with a scullery behind it. There is no bathroom, but there is a tub in the scullery. The WC is outside. The rooms are very small, and the staircase leads direct from the scullery into an upstairs room. The other newer type, semi-detached and slightly larger, has usually three bedrooms, a front room downstairs, a kitchen and a scullery, and also a bathroom. The WC is outside. Most of the houses have small backyards, but as the air is polluted with smoke and dust from the nearby steelworks and other factories none of the gardens are cultivated to any extent. During the survey the sanitary inspectors were asked to assess the structural condition of all these houses, taking four broad categories: good, fair, bad, and very bad. In all cases these houses were assessed as fair.

(ii) The old houses on the Broomhill estate were built in 1922 to relieve the most urgent post-1914-war housing shortage. They are built in concrete, and were not designed to be of long duration. In fact, the original life span was assessed as fifteen years. They were scheduled for demolition, and then put into use again because of the continuing housing shortage. They have three bedrooms, two rooms downstairs, a kitchen and a bathroom. The WCs are by the back door. The gardens are of the usual pre-war council house size. The houses are semi-detached. The assessments of the structural conditions of these houses by sanitary inspectors was 'very bad' in one case, 'bad' in fourteen, and 'fair' in only one case.

(iii) The other houses occupied by the research set on the Broomhill estate are of various types. There are either two or three bedrooms, and either one or two rooms downstairs, a kitchen and a bathroom. The WCs are outside the back door. They are semi-detached and have gardens. The rating of the structural conditions by sanitary inspectors was 'good' in one case, 'fair' in seven cases, and 'bad' in one case.

What are the neighbourhoods like around these three groups of houses? What are the people like who are the neighbours of the families described here? How do they get on with one another? Immediate impressions of the three neighbourhoods are very different. The streets in the docks are dominated by smoke and chimney stacks; towards the lower end of the area the cranes and derricks of the docks are visible beyond railway lines and waste land. The little houses are grey and drab, there are no trees, and what grass there is grows wild here and there on patches of waste ground. The air is heavy with smoke and dust. The group of concrete houses on the Broomhill estate are drab, too; there is hardly a house without broken windows, and most of them have large cracks on the surface which have been temporarily patched up. But the gardens with green hedges and the purer air form a redeeming feature. Very few of the gardens are looked after, however; most of them consist of a patch of wild grass, and often rubbish is strewn all over. The other houses on the estate are much pleasanter. The gardens are better looked after, and the survey families do not live in close proximity to one another.

In an attempt to get a cross-section of impressions of the three neighbourhoods, the people best acquainted with them (sanitary inspectors, health visitors, and, when available, social workers) were asked to assess them as 'good', 'fair', 'poor', or 'very poor'. It was pointed out that the general background for all areas was working-class, and that the assessment was to be made within this setting. The assessment was to apply to the immediate neighbourhood of the families, that is the half-dozen or so houses on each side. This was done to ensure that variations in 'tone' within a street were properly gauged. The results showed a good deal of agreement between the various workers, whose assessments were made independently, although on the whole sanitary inspectors tended to rate a little higher than health visitors and social workers. The general opinion concerning the docks and the concrete houses on Broomhill was that the neighbourhoods were 'poor to very poor'; and the rest of the Broomhill estate was generally considered to be fair.

In a neighbourhood that is generally assessed as being a poor one, it might be expected that the research families would not be considered as deviant in their way of living as they would be in a better neighbourhood. This is an opinion frequently voiced by people who advocate a housing policy of segregation of such families. The evidence collected in the course of the survey is too scant to form a basis of any firm generalizations. It does, however, suggest that an aggregation of low standard families is desirable neither from the point of view of the families themselves, nor from the point of view of the social workers who have dealings with them. Furthermore, it appears that in a neighbourhood that is not too aspiring very low-standard families will settle down and be accepted by their neighbours if they are not in close proximity to one another. The nine families who lived in newer houses on Broomhill seemed to manage, with the exception of two whose very difficult behaviour would upset any neighbours however undemanding in general housekeeping standards. One is a family whose cruel treatment of the mother's step-children over a number of years was well known. The parents were twice convicted of wilful neglect of their children. The health visitor reported: 'The head teacher heard the children were begging . . . Pam reported to be frequently thrown out by her step-mother, crying bitterly. The mother's language is foul. Feeling is strong in the vicinity about these children and the treatment they receive.' The second case was a family whose two eldest sons were very out of hand. Neighbours complained frequently and eventually handed in a petition to the housing department asking for the family to be removed. It said that 'since these people have been living here, their two eldest sons have practically terrorized the neighbourhood, caused untold damage by running over gardens, throwing stones, etc. and should anyone attempt to remonstrate with them, they are treated to a fine sample of obscene language both from the boys and their parents'. The ten families living in the docks also managed reasonably well with their neighbours, with the exception of one who lived next door to a tenant who is buying his house from the corporation, and who sent a note to the housing department complaining about 'the children throwing rubbish of all descriptions into my backyard, and any request to stop it is completely ignored'. It appears that difficulties are likely to arise if standards of neighbours are considerably higher. This was certainly obvious in the case of two families who lived in very much better neighbourhoods. One of them lived on a post-war housing estate which has a considerably higher general standard than Broomhill. They had been living there for about a year when I visited them. I found all their children indoors, although it was a fine day during the Easter holidays. The mother complained that she could not send them out to play because the neighbours were so unfriendly. The other family were in a council house the garden of which ran down to the gardens of privately-owned houses. A letter of complaint was received by the housing department from the estates firm who owned the property at the back pointing out that the children were throwing rubbish across and causing damage to the roof of one of their houses. The welfare officer of the housing department also received complaints from neighbours who said that the father 'is continually drunk and causes frequent scenes in the house'.

It is interesting to compare the mothers' comments on their neighbours with those of the neighbours. The mother of the family who were the cause of a petition by others in the street was quite unaware of any tension in the neighbourhood. She said she liked her house and the people around her, and she did not wish to move. The mother who had been convicted of child neglect, on the other hand, was well aware of her neighbours' criticism. She said she had put in for a transfer; she did not like people around her, and 'found the garden too big to manage'. The family on the new housing estate felt very much ostracized; the others were apparently unaware of tensions.

The group of old concrete houses on Broomhill, however, tells a different story. It is in this area that the heaviest concentration of research families was found. Sixteen families live there in close proximity to other unsatisfactory tenants and socially maladjusted people. The area consists of about 120 houses which are laid out in a square, the central part of which is also built up. There are two adjoining streets of similar character. The houses, built of concrete, were originally intended to have a fifteen-year life span, which expired in 1937. They are classified as 'sub-standard', and the housing department is fully aware of the necessity of scheduling this area for slum clearance. Four families of the research set came here straight from a squatters' camp, and another two from the local authority's welfare accommodation for homeless people. The others had been in rooms previously and had been considerably overcrowded. It is only since about 1950, when the squatters' camps were closed down, that this area has become a reception centre for families considered unfit for ordinary houses. The impact on the old residents has been such that by now most of them have asked for and received transfers to other areas. The district has become known for the complexity of its social problems. The health visitors' comments in reports give an indication of their nature:

'The children are poorly dressed, dirty, and have no pants on, or shoes, or socks. This is common on the square.'

'Since being at the present address the family has had coal pinched, electric meter broken, and windows smashed.'

'Father used to go into a widow's house nearby and was seen leaving early in the morning. She had an illegitimate child and said the father was a sailor . . . but is it a "red light" house?'

The probation officers' reports contain many descriptions of events on the square; the two examples following give an idea of activities there:

'Mother said they had a row with the ——'s again, because Barbara called Ann a nigger because Ann had kicked her. Marion gave an account of their respective mothers smacking each other's faces and pulling each other's hair, but says they are friends again now.'

'Father threw a bottle at a group of boys playing near his home. The bottle struck a lamp-post and one of the boys sustained a deep cut on his index finger . . . The boy's evidence: "I don't know why he threw the bottle at us as we weren't doing anything to annoy him." Father said: "I didn't mean to hurt him. I meant to frighten him away as we have had a lot of windows broken".'

The comments made by the probation officers in their reports point to the particular problems they have to face in the area:

'The square and adjoining streets are corporation property where large families with low incomes have been housed in old concrete type houses with low rents. The result has unfortunately been that a large number of juvenile delinquents live in close proximity to each other.'

'The square is a particularly notorious black spot for crime and delinquency; it houses many of Seaport's problem families.'

Not only is this area a difficult one from the point of view of the health visitor, the social worker, the probation officer, and the housing department, but officers of the NAB also find that the problems of the unemployed become more complex with increasing numbers of local residents out of work. These patterns of behaviour are quickly adopted by newcomers. There are very few men in regular work in this area, and of the sixteen research families only two had a good work record.

Furthermore, not even the tenants themselves are happy in their surroundings. When I interviewed the parents I found that only three families thought the place was 'alright'. One mother said: 'It's alright as long as I keeps myself to myself, otherwise there is murder'. Ten families disliked the square and tried to get moved. Two families, who were part of the original pilot survey, had not been asked. A letter written by a mother to the housing department conveys some of the tension experienced by the inhabitants:

'. . . My children and I are terrified of living in the square, as there is constant fighting between people here . . . I cannot let the children even go out to play as there are a number of children here who terrorize the neighbourhood. My oldest boy who is thirteen is even frightened to go to school . . . The children are continually breaking windows in other people's houses and tormenting the old people around here . . . I have to take the children out all day on Saturdays and Sundays . . . I am afraid to leave my house empty in this district.'

Another letter, written by a father, complains about the neighbours:

'. . . the family next door has been very bad towards us in the past. But last night my wife was hit by the girl next door, and the police was called in. Please can you advise or help in any way to try and sort this out as my wife cannot live in peace . . .'

The following letter was written by a mother shortly after moving into the square:

'. . . and beleave me if I knew before I took the house how they were in the square I would not af took the house for we cannot have any peace there and we are not used to the carring on of the children. Will you please consider my case . . .'

It is quite obvious that in every respect the practice of segregating and grouping sub-standard families in this manner has been a failure. The problems of the individual family cannot be tackled satisfactorily by health visitors and social workers, as they are unable to work against area patterns. Moreover, marginal families are induced to adopt ways of living on moving into the area which were previously alien to them. Old residents with a higher standard are exposed to continuous strain. Beyond that the area gains a bad reputation which brings with it an unjust stigma for many of its residents. The Central Housing Advisory Committee in its report on Unsatisfactory Tenants (1955) says:

'The segregation of unsatisfactory tenants by placing them in groups of houses specially set aside for them was condemned in the first report of this sub-committee on "The Management of Municipal Housing Estates" (HMSO 1939) and we see no reason to dissent from the views then expressed . . . We are aware of the discomfort and even unhappiness which a bad neighbour can cause and of the need therefore of some degree of isolation for the most difficult families. We believe that this is best achieved by the use of individual houses so situated that the behaviour of the occupants will affect other people as little as possible, and that though two or three such houses might be near each other, a greater number will only hinder the work of rehabilitation. Much evidence has been presented to us which suggests that some form of "Family casework service" is needed if effective help is to be brought to the type of family with whom this report deals . . . There is much substance in the argument that the basis of successful work of this kind is the relationship established between the family and one worker, to whom the family as a whole would look, not for advice and admonition, or even material help, so much as for the practical demonstration of how they may gradually overcome their difficulties by their own efforts. This conception owes much to example set by the Family Service Units.'

Although family casework is not the direct responsibility of a housing department, it is important to draw attention to it when discussing the proper placing of sub-standard families on a housing estate. Only too frequently is this aspect of rehabilitative work forgotten when families affected by slum clearance schemes are rehoused. The careful placing of sub-standard families in new neighbourhoods with a high degree of toleration and avoiding segregated grouping will not be successful unless it is accompanied by a remedial service.

We have, so far, not looked at the fourteen families who have private landlords. The information obtained concerning their housing was necessarily scantier than for the council tenants. We did not want to approach landlords and we could not gauge reactions from neighbours. Most of the information about them comes from the interviews I had with the families.

The families are fairly widely dispersed over the older wards of the city. The houses are all terraced, mostly stone, such as are common in the central parts of Seaport. There are no bathrooms in any of them, but tubs were fitted in the sculleries of two houses. The WCs are all outside, close to the back door. Cold water could be drawn from a tap in the sculleries; there was no hot-water system anywhere. As mentioned before, the degree of crowding was higher than for tenants of council houses; the average density per room was two persons. The information concerning rents was obtained before the Rent Act of 1957 had effect, and is based on statements made by the fathers or mothers to me. The average rent paid by the group was £1 0s 2d per week; the lowest actual rent was 10s 0d and the highest was £1 10s 0d.

Sanitary inspectors, health visitors and social workers assessed the immediate neighbourhoods; and the general comment was 'fair to poor'. But here again, as with council tenants, the sanitary inspectors considered the areas to be rather nicer than the health visitors. The sanitary inspectors also assessed the structural conditions of the fourteen houses and found them all to be either 'poor' or 'very poor'. These impressions are also borne out on reading probation officers' and other workers' reports, such as the following:

'The house is old and dilapidated, four of the rooms are un-inhabitable, and the whole family (parents and ten children) live in the remaining four rooms. The house is damp in the extreme and lacking in comfort.'

Here is a newspaper report of one of the families:

'At the time it was raining, and a tin had been placed in the bedroom under a hole in the roof to catch the rain.'

One family was buying the house in which they had lived as tenants for many years. Both parents are known to the local authority as borderline mental defectives. After signing the contract they found that they had to see to their own repairs, of which the house was badly in need. When I visited I found the kitchen floor boards rotting and repairs had just been arranged for. This family got into considerable debt, and they have since had to leave the house. It seems that this type of family is better looked after by a corporation landlord; at least ignorance would not be exploited. Furthermore, repairs are seen to, there are boilers to provide hot water, and in the newer houses there are bathrooms which are essential for families with young children. Housing should be considered of the nature of a social service and it should be available in the first instance for large families who cannot afford to provide suitable accommodation at ordinary rents.

CHAPTER VI

PERFORMANCE INADEQUACY

1. LIVING CONDITIONS

AS described in Chapter II, the families showing five or more performance-inadequacy symptoms were included in the group which provides the material of the present investigation. The list of performance-inadequacy symptoms contains two that are directly related to living conditions: (i) house scantily equipped, and (ii) house dirty, smelly. Although these two conditions need not always be present, they were actually found in the great majority of families. This does not mean that they are chronic conditions. For instance, I sometimes came across vivid descriptions of extreme squalor, and found, on visiting, that things were not too bad. Sometimes this change could be explained by the time interval between a description contained in a file and the visit. Material changes had occurred in the interval. This was particularly obvious with some of the older families. The mothers, now beyond child-bearing, had more time and energy to concentrate on housekeeping, and some of the older children were at work and adding to the family income. In one case the change was due to official pressure. The mother was put on probation for neglect of her children, and for the period of supervision living conditions were considerably better than before. As it turned out, however, deterioration set in soon after the end of probation, and she has again been charged with neglect. In a few cases conditions improved during short periods when the mother had outside assistance. The prevailing conditions described in this chapter are not necessarily either permanent or inherent in the character of the persons who make up the household. The interpretation of the observations set out below is indeed complex; the causes range from the apathy of an over-burdened and over-tired mother to a pathological condition of a personality that unconsciously creates squalor as a justification of the self.

The evidence for these performance inadequacies had to be collected from various workers in the field. Sometimes they are heavily loaded with judgmental comments. These have not been cut out, as it was found more valuable to have the genuine eye-witness report. In the final analysis it is equally important to gauge correctly the worker's exasperation with the unco-operative client, since this exasperation in turn affects the client's attitude. The workers involved are members of the public health, housing, and children's departments; probation officers; NSPCC officials; teachers; and the staff of the child guidance clinic.

The following excerpts are taken from health visitors' notes. (The case numbers quoted also appear in the Tables on pp. 42-44 and 169-171.)

Case 17.   In the back room old mattresses and bedding right up to the ceiling. Middle bedroom one double bed for all the boys (5) covered with old clothes. In the front bedroom all the girls (4)—old clothes, too, for covering. Back room downstairs filled with rubbish, pram had coal in it, the stuffing of upholstered furniture, etc.

Case 11.   Mother's brother also in the house, has ulcerated legs, micturates over chairs and floor, sleeps on two chairs in kitchen.

Case 4.   Furniture in appalling condition. No seating accommodation for meals.

Case 38.   I was almost anaesthetized with smell of urine.

The housing department makes periodic inspections of unsatisfactory tenants, and some of the descriptions are given here:

Case 45.   Very dirty conditions. Pantry used as coal house. Rubbish strewn over rear garden. Tenant's children in appalling conditions—faces and hands practically covered with dirty sores. Matted hair, no feet covering.

Case 38.   . . . whole property in a disgraceful condition, walls badly soiled, furniture a very poor standard . . . Bedding very dirty, walls verminous. On opening the children's bedroom I

found it impossible to enter owing to the revolting smell . . .
Two single beds with filthy bedding, and floor covered in
excreta. Children in neglected and dirty condition. Owing to
nausea I was unable to continue the inspection.

Case 24. The house is in a deplorable state. No living-room
doors, windows smashed, passage wall plaster knocked out,
brick and mortar showing. Generally dirty conditions.

Case 13. Very dirty conditions. Bedding filthy. Could not distinguish sheets from army blankets.

Case. 3. Appalling conditions in the house. One empty bedroom used as a latrine.

Case 2. Heavy smell over entire household. Walls in filthy
conditions. Bedding very meagre. Suspect vermin. Garden neglected, coalhouse used for rubbish. Lavatory seat broken. There
was no fire in the living room, and the four children (two of
whom were without shoes or socks, one in a dirty vest and
another in an old waistcoat) were actually sitting in the fire-
place for the obvious purpose of getting a little warmth. There
were no coats or any such material evident that could possibly
be used for bedcovering, therefore I can only assume that they
sleep in what they were wearing at the time of my visit.

Case 41. Living room: a picture of indescribable chaos. Floor
filthy. Accumulations of dirt and rubbish everywhere. A corner
of the room had been set aside for the dog and her litter of
puppies for use as a kennel. This is boarded approximately three
foot high, and occupies one and a half square yards . . . Very
offensive smell in back bedroom . . . bed verminous, cot filthy.
WC in filthy state. This is undoubtedly due to the tenant not
insisting on the flush being regularly used.

(Six months later) Front room unfurnished, but floor and walls
badly soiled. Pigeons were being kept in the room.

(Five months later) I suspect that a chicken is housed in the
living accommodation. WC pan choked . . . caused by tenant
having dropped a cup into pan which lodged in trap. Forty-two
small window panes were found to be broken.

The Medical Officer of Health gave evidence in a neglect case
(20) in the following words:

I found the whole house in an extremely filthy, untidy and neglectful condition . . . I found partially dried human faeces on floor, vomitus on blanket and mattress of one bed, and evidence of frequent soaking, filth and remains of food on the floor. Only two beds in use . . .

The two following extracts are from probation officers:

Case 51. Mother's living room always filthy, with no attempt at home comforts. She cooks on an open firegrate. Table thick with grease, never covered. Not a decent chair in the house, and children usually eat standing up . . . The place smells abominably.

Case 17. I spent some time knocking (9.30 a.m.) . . . Margery said her Mother and Mary were in bed . . . After a long time Mary came in filthy clothes, she was very dirty and had obviously just got up . . . Place filthy . . . TV set still there . . . in the back room a bare table had remains of breakfast of bacon and cornflakes . . . Mary said mother too ill to come down. I went upstairs to find her on an old mattress with baby in her arms and three small fully-clothed children sleeping higgledy-piggledy on the bed . . . The children's bedroom had a huge bed with a smelly overlay and old rags as coverings . . .

Of the many descriptions of home conditions given as evidence in neglect cases by NSPCC inspectors the following one has been selected:

Case 37. The midwife called while I was at the home, and I learnt that no provision had been made for the coming child despite the fact that the pre-maternity grant had been received and spent . . . I found that four of the chairs and one double bed had been chopped up and used for firewood. I also found that the top of a brand new washing board had been chopped up and that floorboards had been taken up from the front bedroom, small bedroom, back bedroom, bathroom, and landing, and these had all been chopped up and used for the fire. The man was not working and could easily have gone to the woods and collected sticks . . . a pawn ticket for a pair of flannelette sheets, a quilt, a pair of towels, bolster, and four pillows at 12s 6d. Next day Father received £3 8s od National Assistance but did not get the things out of pawn . . . When Father came in I questioned him and he admitted that he had cursed at the midwife and told her that she was getting £50 a week for her —— job, and all she had to do was to do her bloody work and not find fault with the conditions of his home. When the midwife came to the home Mother was in labour and she was in bed with the other three children. The three children had to be bundled upstairs and laid on a cold bed with no coverings to get them out of the way. The midwife had to get coal from next door to have a fire to get hot water . . .

It is not possible to draw conclusions concerning the parents' mentality from such evidence. To do this would need the insight and special skills of psychiatric workers. This chapter is entirely concerned with giving an indication of prevailing conditions. It is important to remember that such a picture is by no means a static one, that changes have been found and recorded in the course of the investigation, sometimes for the better; in some cases, however, for the worse. No attempt is made to measure such changes, since the primary aim of this investigation has been to ascertain the criminal activities of the children who grow up under conditions such as are described.

2. USE OF WELFARE SERVICES

It may be asked how is it possible, with all the services offered in the welfare state, to live on such an extremely low level? Under the Health Service Act a provision is made for every newborn baby to be visited by a health visitor at three-monthly intervals during the first year, and after that twice a year until school age. If the health visitor feels that more frequent visiting is advisable she can use her discretion. Additional advice and help is offered to young mothers and babies in weekly baby clinics. Evidence collected during the investigation indicates that these services are not properly used by the mothers of the research set. The following quotations are examples of the type of problems encountered; they are taken from health visitors' notes.

Case 42. A neighbour told health visitor that the mother dresses up and goes out at night, leaving the children alone in the house. The children called the neighbour in one night—

conditions were shocking. Mother won't allow health visitor to enter.

Case 14. Mother does not take Sandra to the Rheuma clinic.

Case 30. Mother failed to attend dental clinic appointments. Mother has no books for welfare foods.

Case 34. Freddie does not attend clinic for heart.

Case 28. Mother refused to attend ante-natal clinic.

Case 47. NSPCC inspector took William to eye clinic, but parents would not co-operate. William is to wear patch and glasses, but does not.

Case 23. Pamela does not attend asthma clinic, although sent for twice. Yvonne cannot have glasses until mother can find her identity number.

Case 3. Mother does not see to Pamela's orthopaedic boots. NSPCC inspector had to take her to be fitted.

Case 7. When children had scabies father refused to let them go to clinic. Mother refused to send children to clinic for head cleansing.

Case 27. NSPCC inspector had to take Queenie to ENT clinic.

Case 6. Father won't allow treatment of umbilical hernias of two daughters.

Case 33. Enuresis clinic: no co-operation with mother, who keeps losing forms.

Case 12. Father refused to let children have X-rays for suspected TB. (An elder sister contracted TB.) Children had to be fetched by ambulance one day when father was out.

The following observation was made by a probation officer:

Case 50. Edward was involved in a road accident when three years old and sustained a fractured skull. Extremely deaf, never received treatment.

The failure to make arrangements for confinement is observed many times: here are two examples from health visitors' records:

Case 3. Mother pregnant, due this month. Has made no arrangement for confinement.

Case 21. Mother made no arrangement for confinement, or clothes. She has only six napkins.

Similar negative attitudes to other services are recorded.

Case 23. Mental health liaison officer reported visits to mother on three occasions to persuade her to go to the psychiatric out-patients' clinic, but failed.

Case 24. Martin referred to child guidance clinic. Failed to co-operate, mother failed to attend. Case closed.

Case 1. Child guidance clinic failed to obtain any co-operation from the parents when previous requests for examination of other members of the family have been made.

Case 26. Mother refused to let Henry go to Residential Special School.

Case 33. Mary was recommended for Residential Special School, but father refused to let her go.

Case 25. Father did not apply for free school meals for his children, as it appeared he did not want to declare his income.

The following report was made by the School Medical Service:

Case 20. I saw the three children with their father a year ago and requested free dinners for them as a result of their neglected and poor physical appearance. Since both parents were working they were asked to pay, and the children were soon having their midday meal at home again . . . Definite evidence of malnutrition.

Apparently it is difficult to get home helps to work in households with very low standards:

Case 48. Attempts have been made to get a home help, but City Hall reports that home helps would not go there because of the number of children and dirt.

If a home help is found who is willing to work under such conditions difficulties with the parents are likely to arise. This is hardly avoidable, since it is the job of the home help to clean up within the time given to her. It is in the nature of her job that she imposes certain standards for which the family may not be ready:

Case 17. Mother did not want home help—she was turned away when she came to do the washing one day.

Case 29. Father resents 'officials' and would not allow his wife to have a home help when she was confined last.

Case 3. Home help will be supplied on condition that this is part of rehabilitation service. Home help will be paid time and a half. (Health Department file) Improvement maintained materially. Home help did a lot. But neighbours' comments depressed mother. (Children's Department) Home help no longer sent there, the family regretted having her. Apparently gossip had reached mother, and she suspected home help of originating this. (Children's Department.)

It is obvious from quotations such as the above that these services are of a type that hardly fit the conditions of this kind of family.

3. FAMILY PLANNING

The health visitors were asked whether they had discussed birth control with any of the mothers. In twenty-three cases the health visitors said they had not; fourteen mothers were considered 'too dim' to raise such a subject, and nine mothers were known to be Roman Catholics. Six mothers were sterilized after setting up large families, and two mothers were on the waiting list for sterilization. Four mothers had been advised in a family-planning clinic, but pregnancies had occurred soon afterwards. There were three mothers who had recently been advised, too soon to know how successfully. Four mothers had been approached by their health visitors but had not shown any interest. Three families are not visited by health visitors, one woman was divorced, and two families had one parent only through death. In the four remaining families I did not discuss the subject with the health visitor. In talking to the mothers myself many different reasons were given by the woman who did not at once turn down the idea of family planning out of principle. They may have been nothing but rationalizations, but the difficulties are real enough. The clinics were too far to visit regularly; all the children of under-school age would have to be taken along; they had no decent underclothes to show to nurse; to buy the equipment was silly when they had not enough money for more essential things; and so on. There are other very real difficulties. There is no privacy in the home, and the parental bed is usually shared with some of the younger children.

Similar impressions were gained by Stephens (1945), who also adds that the fathers were generally quite uninterested in the question of family limitation. These impressions are substantiated by the doubts voiced by Professor Madge in his introduction to a report on the progress of a Birmingham Family Planning Clinic (see Florence, 1956). The report shows that over a lengthy period of time less than half the clients persevered in using contraceptives. A follow-up of those who had given up the use of contraceptives showed that there were a large number of unintended pregnancies, especially among manual labourers. Professor Madge concludes that 'a safe and acceptable alternative is urgently needed, even in a country like Britain where standards of education and housing are relatively high'. These are the comments on the findings of a clinic that deals with the general run of the population; they are even more to the point in a consideration of family planning for people whose living standards are much below the average.

A health visitor with a good deal of experience and good relationships with her clients summed up her impressions in the following way: 'Many mothers in the area can't be bothered with birth control, perhaps because they are too apathetic, too listless and tired to be bothered about anything. Perhaps they don't understand how to fit the cap, although they are shown in the clinic.' This health visitor is often asked by mothers how to 'get rid of it', when they have become pregnant. A number of mothers are not shy of mentioning to her that they have been successful with abortion. Another health visitor, working in a different area, said that a good many of the 'less respectable' mothers resorted to all sorts of methods to terminate the pregnancy. They would not give details to the health visitor because they are fully aware of the legal consequences. If questioned about miscarriages they would say that they had taken a double dose of quinine because of the 'flu. There are other methods in common use, some of which have been known for generations, and have been used widely in the surrounding rural areas.

3. ATTITUDES TO EDUCATION

Similar difficulties of co-operation are reported in the educational field. In a previous chapter school-attendance figures were given which showed a very high incidence of frequent absences from school. Only about 20 per cent were found to have normal attendance records. Some quotations from the case records will throw some light on the problems involved.

Case 24. Peter filthy dirty at school and referred by nurse. Now mother keeps him at home. (Health Visitor.)

Case 41. Head teacher sent note to mother to change her son's trousers. The boy has not been to school since; this was two weeks ago. (Verbal information from teacher.)

Case 50. Margaret and Anne are kept home from school to help in the house. (Probation Officer.)

Case 19. Promises were frequently made by both parents but none of them ever materialized. The mother was always evasive and plausible, and it is felt that neither parent had made much attempt to encourage Richard to go to school. (Probation Officer.)

Case 16. From January 31st to April 19th Carol was absent from school because of trouble at home. (Head Teacher.)

Case 51. Mother argues that if Jack gets to school by 10 a.m. it is quite satisfactory. (Child Guidance Clinic.)

Case 5. The children are often not in school before 10 to 10.30. Mother does not get up. (Head Teacher.)

Case 2. Mother allows children to come and go as they like. Lack of home training and discipline retard the children's educational progress . . . John's absences have had a serious effect on his work. If he had attended regularly his standard would have been considerably higher. (Head Teacher.)

Case 44. Mary produces batches of medical certificates to cover her absences from school which are sent to the school attendance office, and nothing can be done. (School Attendance Office.)

Case 3. No truancy, but wilful refusal to go to school. He said the headmaster is always asking for dinner money and he hasn't got it. (Probation Officer.)

Case 40. John—very low educational attainments and persistently absent. Mother has sent to me for assistance to get John into school . . . Her idea is that two or three boys might forcibly persuade that school is a desirable occupation. (Head Teacher.)

Case 48. I later saw Bobby on the bus—asked why he was scared. He said he was having a week off school because his gran had died. Mother had told him to get the bus in case the 'Boardy' (School Attendance Officer) would see him. He seemed to relish telling me this and confided in me as a fellow conspirator. (Probation Officer.)

Case 4. It is significant that the child is kept home from school and encouraged in various other minor anti-social behaviour by the mother who makes all excuses, mostly lies, to account for her non-attendance. (Child Guidance Clinic.)

The above quotations, like those on the use of the welfare

services, show elements of aggressive reactions to official approaches, as well as apathetic attitudes on the side of the parents. Both attitudes, however, have the same result, that of preventing the child from benefiting fully from his educational opportunities. Schooling is not an activity that is valued highly.

5. SPENDING PATTERNS

The chapter dealing with parents' health and incomes has given ample evidence of the very real struggle practically all the families have in making ends meet. It has been shown that in many cases only a person with very great self-discipline and good intelligence would be able to manage, and that in a number of cases even such a person could not avoid falling into debt. These are primarily the families on long-term State-maintained allowances for whom the 'wage stop' rule is working, and whose actual income is below subsistence level. It also includes families with more than six or seven children whose fathers' earnings do not exceed £8 10s od per week. Under such conditions it is difficult, if not impossible, to discuss evidence of 'mis-spending'. Where indeed is the line to be drawn between what is necessary and what can be done without? If the week's income is not sufficient to meet the necessary in any case, the temptation to spend it on the inessential is so much the greater. In addition, the offers of house-to-house salesmen are harder to turn down when the needs and wishes of the housewife are never, or only rarely, met, and when the housewife never has a chance to pay cash in a shop for a desired article. Payment on instalments even for small articles is the pattern, and accumulation of debts is unavoidable when there is not enough to meet essential needs.

The evidence concerning debts is based almost entirely on the interviews I had with the parents, and it is, therefore, largely uncorroborated. It may be assumed, however, that any statements concerning debts are genuine, and that the element of error may come in with understatement rather than overstatement. The parents knew that they had nothing to gain from revealing their financial position to me; they would not, therefore, be tempted to exaggerate their state of indebtedness. In some cases there was obvious reluctance to reveal their full debts. Seven families, who were interviewed during a preliminary pilot survey, were not questioned on this topic—its importance emerged only in the course of the pilot survey. In five other cases it was not possible to continue the interview to the point of discussing finances. In one of them a neighbour was present; in another the mother, a mentally defective woman, seemed unable to put her case coherently; in a third case the eldest daughter (aged 22) was interviewed, as the mother was out; in a fourth case the interview was with the father, who was not willing to discuss money matters; and in the fifth case I did not ask any further questions after finding that the mother had been continuously unreliable in her statements about matters of fact already known to me. This mother was at the time on probation for neglect of her children, and her intention in the interview was to show that she was a very good mother indeed.

Since the nature of the subject under discussion is a very personal one, in the sense of revealing failure or success in budgeting, no attempt is made to analyse the interview results statistically. The response 'no debts' may mean either what it says, or 'I am not going to admit to you that I have been unable to keep clear of debts'. Some women, however, took the line that, however hard they struggled, it was impossible to make ends meet. Eighteen women spoke of more or less heavy debts which it was difficult to eradicate. The following case is typical:

I owes 14s od to the lady next door, and £1 12s od on another bill, and county court debts of £10 and another £7 . . . They can put father in prison for that (starts crying) . . . I also owes approved school for Tommy . . .

Of the eighteen women who discussed their debts five were assessed as 'mis-spenders' by two or more social workers. One father was described as a heavy gambler, and there was in fact a conviction for 'resorting to common gaming house'. In two cases the fathers were described as heavy drinkers. The father of another family, who is described as a psychopathic personality by the psychiatrist who treated him while in a mental hospital, is known to buy inessentials at the cost of providing necessities for the family:

Father would buy new things for mother and then let her pay

instalments—things come and go: a dog, budgerigars, a kitchen cabinet, a cocktail cabinet, TV, even a pony . . . The children are badly clad. (Health Visitor.)

In the fifth case there is evidence that the maternity grant on one occasion was used as a deposit for a TV set, and no money was available to provide the necessities for the confinement. In this case there is a continuous shortage of money, and rent arrears were well over £50 in the summer of 1957.

Of the remaining twenty-seven families who would not disclose their financial positions four fathers are known to be heavy drinkers, and in a further two cases both father and mother drink heavily; in one of them, however, it has been observed that the mother has recently left off drinking excessively. In two further families the mothers are described as heavy smokers. In three families there is evidence of habitual gambling: one father had two convictions for resorting to a common gaming house; another father in one instance disposed of the weekly payment of the National Assistance Board and left the family with nothing; and in the third case the mother, a widow, is described by the probation officer as a gambler. 'Mother bets considerably. Anything is turned into money to bet with.'

It is perhaps surprising to find that, out of a total of fifty-two families, only eight fathers have been assessed as heavy drinkers by the social workers acquainted with the families, and only four fathers as gamblers. In the great majority of cases neither of the parents was considered to be excessive in spending habits. This, however, is not the same thing as ability in general budgeting. In a number of cases the mothers were not considered capable of allotting the money to the things considered most important by the health visitors or social workers. But opinions of this kind could not be standardized, and are not included in detail here.

6. CONCLUSIONS

None of the above-mentioned conditions can be taken as inherent or ineradicable characteristics of so-called problem families. As has been explained in the section dealing with methodology (Chapter II), the only practical way of forming a group of families suitable for research purposes was to submit a large number of possible families to a test of performance inadequacy. Those scoring most heavily were included in the research group. The existence of a number of such inadequacies became a definition of the group under investigation. Such a definition may not be acceptable to all workers, and other definitions not including the above-mentioned performance inadequacies may be formulated. For the purpose of the present investigation, however, a certain minimum number of these inadequacies is the requisite for inclusion in the research set. They are not to be considered anything but sociologically ascertainable symptoms of living on a level below that generally acceptable to the community. Any interpretation in psychiatric terms of the aetiology of these inadequacies must be left to those qualified to undertake such interpretations. It is obvious to the sociological observer that these may be manifold. If one wishes to understand the interrelationship, however, between the individual and his social group then it is as important to assess the individual personality as his economic position and his relationship to the various services that are offered to him in the welfare state. It is only too often taken for granted that such services are fully used or fully available to all. The evidence quoted in this chapter indicates that this is not the case. There are indications that sometimes this is due primarily to the failure of the potential consumer to make use of them. But on probing further such failure can no longer be seen in merely negative terms, but it has to be seen, instead, in terms of reactions of the individual to certain experiences in using the social services. The case of the health visitor who does not gain entrance may be a response of the family who cannot accept the health visitor as a trusted adviser, but who see her instead as an official in uniform who is imposing standards, who is judgmental. The home-help service, created to assist housewives in their normal routine while temporarily incapacitated, is unacceptable because the standards expected by the home helps are too high. The school teacher who demands a certain degree of cleanliness drives the parent who cannot comply into an obstinate refusal to co-operate at all.

Sometimes, however, the failure to make use of the services is caused by a lack of understanding of their purpose on the part of the consumer. The case quoted of the father who would not let his children be examined in the chest clinic was coupled with the fear that they would be taken from him, since his wife had died of tuberculosis recently and one elder daughter was in hospital. The reluctance to let the children go to residential schools is often coupled with the fear that they will go for good, or that it is some form of punishment. Failure to keep appointments with clinics is an expression of the low rating of such services in the eyes of some parents, and is very often a lack of understanding of the possible serious consequences of neglecting various ailments.

There are other cases, however, of mothers with several small children born in quick succession, who find it impossible to attend clinics or to see to the various needs arising within the family. The mother, physically worn out, usually badly nourished and full of anxiety concerning the family's material needs, has no energy left, nor time, to dress up and get all the small children ready to accompany her on a visit to the welfare clinic. What, in any case, could she do beyond what she was already doing, what possible use could any advice on baby care be to her? Furthermore, being only too aware of the inadequacies of her ways of living, and her inability to make improvements, how could she be expected to seek advice? The standards expected are much too high, and the necessary resources, material and personal, are not available.

CHAPTER VII

JUVENILE DELINQUENCY: THE FACTS

1. AIMS OF THE INVESTIGATION

The main purpose of the survey was to ascertain the rate of delinquency per child at risk in families exhibiting signs of child neglect, and to compare this rate with the rate of delinquency prevailing in the districts in which these families live. Furthermore, it was hoped to divide the research families into two groups: families with delinquents and families without delinquents. A comparison of the two groups would, it was hoped, shed light on the aetiology of juvenile delinquency.

The results of the investigation showed that juvenile delinquency is part of the pattern of juvenile behaviour in the families whose living conditions have been described. The rate of delinquency is consistently higher than in control groups living in the same neighbourhoods; and it is also equally high among families living in comparative isolation from one another in neighbourhoods with a relatively low rate of delinquency. Furthermore, the investigation showed that the great majority of families who had adolescent children had at least one, and usually more than one, child found guilty of an indictable offence. It was, therefore, not possible to make comparisons between the two groups, as the number of families with adolescent non-delinquent children was insignificant.

2. DEFINITION OF JUVENILE DELINQUENCY

The term juvenile delinquent, as used in this survey, means a boy or girl found guilty by a juvenile court of an indictable offence and certain non-indictable offences of a similar character. A full list of offences is given in the appendix. It also includes boys or girls found guilty of truancy, and children brought to court as beyond control, or as in need of care and protection if the case arose out of delinquent acts of the child. (Other cases of care and protection, arising out of parental neglect, were not included.) These cases, a total of three, were included because we felt that there is no difference in nature between children brought to court after a police investigation, and children brought to court by another party because they have committed delinquencies. The following case illustrates the point:

Charles, born 1945, was committed to care of the local authority under Section 5 (c) Children Act in July, 1955. He was brought before court as being beyond control of his mother. He had been referred previously to the Child Guidance Clinic in February, 1954, for truancy, pilfering, and soiling. He stole money, rent money, stayed out late, on occasions all night. Mother did not know what he did. A child care officer reported: 'His practice of pilfering from Woolworth's has become almost a daily habit, but whether it has become more conspicuous because of its great frequency, or because items which are pilfered are more frequently brought home, it is difficult to say.'

Non-indictable offences which are non-criminal in nature have not been entered, such as traffic offences, trespassing on private property, playing games or having fights in streets. The children convicted of this type of offences therefore appear in this survey as 'non-delinquent'. Furthermore, 'further cases taken into consideration' have not been recorded separately. A single delinquent act is entered, for instance, in the case of a boy who had twenty-eight further cases of breaking, entering, and larceny recorded against him, in addition to the offence for which he was convicted. The figures given below are, therefore, if anything an understatement of the seriousness of the situation. Sometimes stealing at school was mentioned by teachers, or appeared in the files of the Child Guidance Clinic in seven cases which were not proceeded with in court, and these offences have therefore not been included in the survey figures. It must also be remembered that on the average only about 40 per cent of all indictable offences known to the police in Seaport are cleared up. The dark figure of the undetected young offender is bound to be among the group of non-delinquents of our survey.

3. THE CASE MATERIAL

The procedure used for collecting the information was to inspect all existing police records of the children who were over eight years old in January, 1955. The offences of which the children were found guilty were entered, and the type of offence, the date, and treatment ordered by the magistrates was specified. As described in Chapter V, there are three distinct area-groups of families as well as some families who are more widely dispersed. The three groups were found to be in (i) the docks area, (ii) in sub-standard houses on the Broomhill estate, and (iii) in newer houses on the same estate. Two control groups for purposes of comparison were formed in the two areas best known to the police, the docks, and the area of sub-standard houses on Broomhill. In presenting the control-group rates these two groups are lumped together since chi-squared tests have shown that the difference between them are entirely without significance.

A comparison was also made between overall delinquency rates in Seaport for a three-year period as estimated by Grünhut (1956) and those produced during a three-year period by children of the research set. In this comparison the figures are those for indictable offences only, as specified by Grünhut, and they include no cases brought to court as in need of care, nor do they include truancy.

4. THE RESULTS

(A) The overall picture

Of the fifty-two families five had children under eight years only. Another six families had no boys above the age of eight, and as the rate of delinquency among the girls is very much lower, the fact that their girls were non-delinquent gave us no indication of their boys' behaviour when 'at risk', i.e. above eight years old. Another seven families had no boys older than eleven; and they had not appeared in juvenile courts. We were reluctant, however, to include these families in a group of non-delinquents, since our survey showed that the peak ages of entry into delinquency are twelve and thirteen. Whereas only about nine per cent of the boys aged eight were delinquent, about one-quarter of the so far non-delinquent boys became delinquent at the age of twelve, and another one-third make their first appearance in the juvenile court aged thirteen. (For details see Appendix V.) It is not unreasonable to state that the test for the non-delinquent families lies in the period during which their boys pass through the peak ages of entry, twelve and thirteen years. There were only four families with boys over twelve years old who, at the time of the survey, had not appeared in a juvenile court. The remaining thirty families all had at least one delinquent child.

It is interesting to take a closer look at the four families with adolescent boys who had not appeared before a court. The number was too small to make any significant comparisons, but if their children really steered clear of delinquencies, it was worth finding out in which way home conditions differed from those in the other families. The first family consisted of a father and ten children, nine girls and a boy. The mother had died during childbirth, and one of the elder daughters was keeping house at the time of the investigation. At that time the only boy was thirteen, and he had not appeared before a court. He had, however, a shocking school attendance record and he was being watched for a possible prosecution. It was known that he spent a good deal of his time going around with a rag-and-bone man. A year later the father was prosecuted for neglect of his children and sent to prison, and all the children under sixteen are now in the care of the local authority. The second family with non-delinquent adolescent children was one with nine children, the eldest being two girls aged fifteen and sixteen when the survey was on. There were two boys aged eight and twelve. The eldest girl had been committed to the care of the Children's Officer when she had an illegitimate baby at the age of fifteen. There was some fear that the second girl would go the same way, and the family was for that reason visited frequently by a local welfare agency. Neither of the boys had become delinquent by that time. A third family had two children 'at risk', both boys. The elder was aged twelve when the survey was conducted. He is feeble-minded and under close supervision, attending an occupation centre which supplies transport to and from home. The younger brother, aged ten, had no police record either. The fourth family with non-delinquent children had a boy aged fourteen when the survey was on. (This boy has been convicted of delinquencies since the closing date of the survey.) A sister was twelve, and four more children were under nine years old. Although none of these children had appeared in court at the time, the teachers described their behaviour as completely unrestrained; they did not know right from wrong, and took anything they could lay their hands on at school. The youngest boy had to empty his pockets on leaving school every day. It was obvious that none of these four families could serve as exhibiting no signs of delinquency.

On looking at the records of all the families who had children at risk, and especially those with boys aged twelve or over, we gained the impression that it was not a question of which family was non-delinquent, but which child in a delinquency-producing family remained non-delinquent. But even then the rate of delinquency per child at risk was considerably higher than the overall rate for the city, as estimated by Grünhut (1956). He estimated the total juvenile population in the two age groups of 8-13 years, and 14-17 years, and then expressed the number of offences committed during a three-year period as a percentage of the total age group. For the ages 8-13 he found that 50.6 indictable offences had been committed per 1,000 boys, and in the age group 14-17 the number of offences was 67.6 per 1,000 boys. These rates are somewhat above the national averages, which are 39 per 1,000 for age 8-13, and 51 per 1,000 for age 14-17. The three years for which figures were taken were 1948-1950. In trying to compare the overall figures for the city given by Grünhut with the delinquency rates obtained from the research set, the difficulty arose of having only a small number of boys and girls of the requisite age groups. There were on the average forty-five boys aged 8-13 during the period 1953-1955 by whom nineteen offences were committed (indictable offences only), and seventeen boys aged 14-17, by whom eight offences were committed. Expressed in terms comparable with Grünhut's this would give a rate of 422 per 1,000 for boys aged 8-13 and 492 per 1,000 for boys aged 14-17. (As an illustration of the fluctuation to which averages based on such small numbers are subject, it may be mentioned that delinquency rates were higher in 1952, and if the three-year period 1952-1954 had been taken the rates would have been 599 and 746 per 1,000 respectively.)

For girls the national averages as well as those for Seaport are very much lower than the boys' delinquency rates. Grünhut gives as the national average per 1,000 for girls aged 8-13 the figure 3.4 and for girls aged 14-17 the rate is 6.5. The corresponding rates for Seaport as given by Grünhut are 4.5 and 7.9 respectively. As expected, the rates for girls in the research set were very much lower than those for the boys, but they were considerably higher than the national rates. Expressed in terms comparable to Grünhut's the following figures do no more than indicate the order of magnitude of the rate: 97 per 1,000 for the age group 8-13, and 48 per 1,000 for the age group 14-17. (If the three-year period 1952-1954 had been chosen the figures would have been 151 and 107 per 1,000 respectively.)

Although neither of these sets of figures can be taken as anything more than an indication of trends, it was obvious that the rate of delinquency among the research set of boys was about eight times as high for the 8-13 age group as the average for the city, and for 14-17-year-old boys it was over seven times. The girls' rates were about a third of the boys' rates of delinquency; much higher than the national percentages which are in the neighbourhood of ten.

(B) The boys

A comparison of delinquency rates of the research set with those for the city as a whole can give little more than an overall picture. Delinquents are not spread evenly over the city, but they are found in clusters; and in Seaport there are two areas which are particularly well known to the police. One is the area referred to as the group of sub-standard houses on Broomhill, the other one is the docks area. Although not all our families lived there we decided to compare their delinquency rates with those prevailing in these two black areas. We formed two control groups by obtaining a list of all families living in four streets in the docks, a total of 189 houses, and of all families living on the so-called square of Broomhill, a total of 103 houses. Any family so obtained which was already in the research set was extracted, and all children over the age of eight in the remaining families were examined. The control group in the docks contained sixty-two boys and seventy girls at risk, and the group on Broomhill contained sixty-three boys and fifty-two girls. Chi-

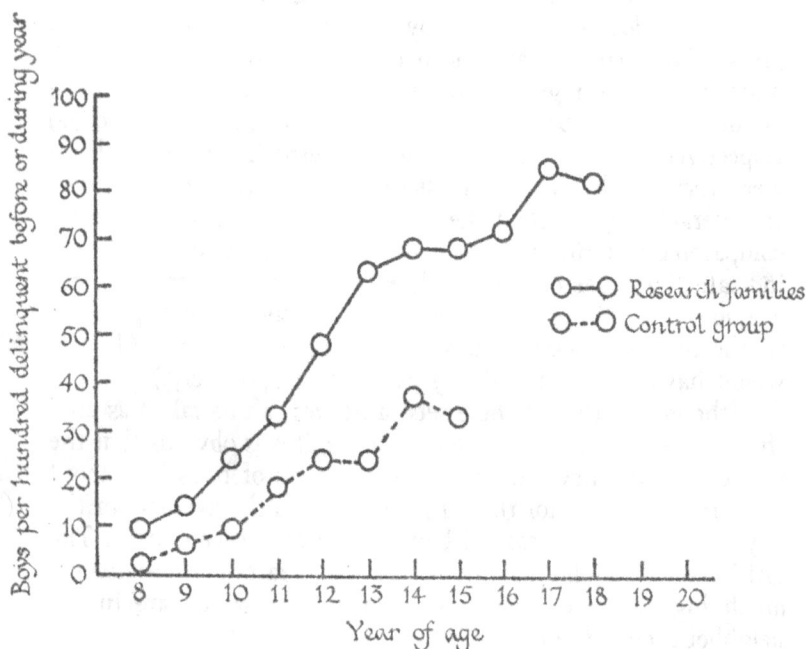

Fig. 3. Cumulative delinquent rate for boys as a function of age, being the number of boys per hundred who have been convicted at some time before or during the year of age stated. The upper curve is for the research families, the lower curve for the control group. Removal of delinquents to approved schools etc reduces the apparent rate at the higher ages, as only children actually in the picture at each age have been counted.

squared tests showed that there was no significant differences in the rates of delinquency in the two control groups, and they were therefore taken together in the comparisons with the research family rates. The research families had ninety-eight boys and ninety-six girls at risk. They, too, did not show any difference in rates according to their places of residence, and they are also presented together as a single group.

The cumulative rate of delinquency of the control boys in these black areas proved to be a much higher one than the estimated averages for the city. (For details see Appendix VI.) But even here the research family boys did worse: their rates were consistently more than double the rates of the controls,

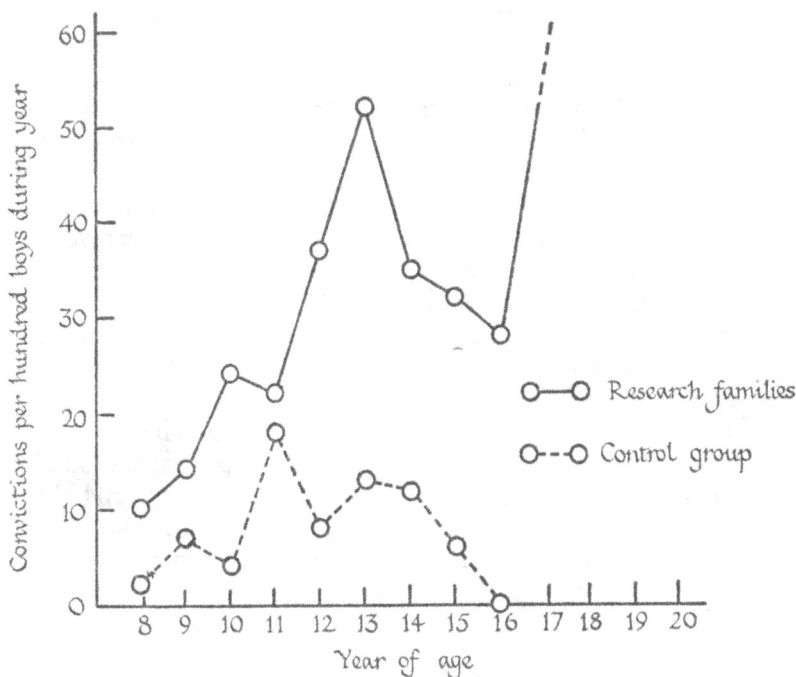

Fig. 4. Delinquency rate (number of convictions per hundred boys in year) as a function of age. The upper curve is for the research families and the lower curve is for the control group.

and this applied equally to research boys living in black areas as to those living in more respectable parts of the city. We found that even at the young age of eight the contrast was already visible: only two per cent of the controls had a conviction, whereas nine per cent of the research set were delinquent. By the time the boys were ten years old, under ten per cent of the controls and a quarter of the research boys had become delinquent. The contrast became greater by the time they were between twelve and thirteen. About a quarter of the control boys had by now become delinquent, but of the research group nearly 65 per cent belonged to the delinquent group. The peak was reached by the controls at the age of fourteen with about a third delinquent. The peak for the research group was reached aged seventeen when well over 80 per cent had put in at least one appearance in a juvenile court and had been convicted of one of the specified offences (fig. 3, p. 118). Taking all ages together we found that fifty-six of the ninety-eight boys at risk in the research set were delinquents, and of the 125 controls thirty-three boys were. On looking at their records of reconvictions, we found that among the fifty-six research boys who were delinquent twenty had been convicted once, and thirty-six two or several times. Of the thirty-three delinquent controls nineteen were convicted once, and fourteen two or several times. The rate of recidivism, as a percentage of delinquents, was 64 per cent in the research set, and 42 per cent among the controls. (The difference is significant at the five per cent level.)

Looking at the delinquency rates, i.e. the number of convictions per hundred boys of age stated (fig. 4, p. 119) we found again that the difference between the research group and the controls was statistically speaking highly significant. (The value of chi-squared was 48.0 with nine degrees of freedom, which is highly significant, falling well outside the normal range of tables of chi-squared.) We found that at the age of ten the number of convictions of research boys was twenty-four per hundred, whereas of the controls it was four per hundred. At the age of thirteen the research group had well over fifty convictions per hundred boys, whereas the controls had thirteen per hundred. (All details referred to on these pages are given in the Appendices VII and VIII.)

What kind of offences did the research group boys commit? The type and the distribution was very similar to juvenile offences in general. Larceny headed the list with a total of ninety-seven offences; of which forty-eight were unspecified and thirty-four took place 'in dwelling'. Shoplifting had been undertaken on seven occasions. Breaking and entering was the second most frequent offence with forty-one cases. There were twenty-four cases of malicious or wilful damage, two cases of robbery, one committed by an 11-year-old, the other by a 16-year-old boy, two cases of receiving, one case of burglary by a 17-year-old boy, and one case of assault with intent to rob. There was, in addition, one case of taking and driving away a motor-car, three cases of larceny of growing fruit, and three cases where fit person orders were made after delinquencies. There were also twenty-one convictions for truancy. (For details see Appendix IX.)

(C) The girls

Girls are not as delinquent as boys. Over the country as a whole the ratio of delinquent girls to delinquent boys is in the neighbourhood of one to ten. On investigating the girls in the research families, however, a different picture emerged. On the whole the rate of delinquency among them is very similar to that of the control boys, and in the teenage range the research girls are rather more delinquent than the control boys. At age twelve eight delinquencies were committed per hundred control boys, and ten per hundred research girls. Aged thirteen the rate for the control boys was thirteen, and for the research girls twenty. It remained high for the girls through adolescence, whereas for the controls the rate tapered off. (See Appendix VII.) The average delinquency rate of the research-family girls aged 8-16 inclusive was around 10 per cent per year, whereas that of the control boys in the same age group is only 8 per cent. (The research family boys had a rate of 28 per cent per year.) The cumulative delinquent rate is perhaps even more interesting in a discussion of the sex ratio, as it shows the percentage of all children at risk who have become delinquent by the time they have reached the age tabulated. As the group of children was formed on the basis of education department lists, no details were obtainable for children older than sixteen. For that reason a comparison is made for the sixteen-year-old group. More than two-thirds of the research family boys had become delinquent by that age, whereas about one-third of both control boys and research-family girls had become delinquent. (See Appendix VI.)

The peak age of entry into delinquency for the research girls was thirteen, when 15 per cent of the so-far non-delinquent girls appeared in court. The number of convictions per hundred girls was low up to age twelve, when it rose to ten. At age thirteen there were twenty convictions per hundred girls, but the total number of convictions at the higher ages was too small to make generalizations. As an indication of trends it may suffice to say that they fluctuated between eleven and twenty per hundred girls. (See Appendix VII.)

The girls committed thirty-two offences of larceny, of which seventeen were unspecified, nine were shop-lifting offences, and six were committed in dwellings. Eight girls had convictions for breaking into shops, houses, or schools; they were between nine and fourteen years old. A sixteen-year-old and a seventeen-year-old had convictions for assault, one of them also a conviction for using obscene language. Two girls were caught stealing growing fruit, and there were fifteen supervision orders for truancy. (For details see Appendix IX.)

(D) Summary

The results showed that the rate of delinquency among families exhibiting signs of child neglect was eight times as high as the general rate for boys in Seaport, as estimated by Grünhut (1956). It was also well over twice the rate prevailing in families other than the research families who lived in the closest proximity to them in two districts of Seaport which are well known to the police. Furthermore, the research families living in relative isolation in low-delinquency areas of the city show a rate of delinquency similar to that of those living in clusters in high-delinquency areas. The rate of recidivism for delinquent boys of the research families is higher than that of the controls by about a third. The ratio of female to male delinquents in the research families is something like one to three, which is much higher than the national average of about one to ten. The rate of delinquency of the research family girls is similar to that of the control boys. The numbers and percentages given in these pages refer to detected offences only, and it must be remembered that only about 40 per cent of indictable offences are detected annually in Seaport. The dark figure of the undetected offender is bound to be hidden in the non-delinquent group.

Taking into consideration that at the time of the investigation only four research families with adolescent boys had steered clear of the juvenile court and, furthermore, that the rate of delinquency is consistently high independent of residence, we may draw the conclusion that juvenile delinquency is part of the pattern of juvenile behaviour among families exhibiting signs of child neglect.

CHAPTER VIII

JUVENILE DELINQUENCY:
AN INTERPRETATION

1. THE FACTORS AFFECTING THE CHILDREN'S UPBRINGING

(A) *General considerations*

THE high rate of juvenile delinquency found in the research set of families points the way to a fuller understanding of one variety of delinquent behaviour among children. Here is a group of families, living in various areas, some in clusters, others in isolation from one another, some living in districts well known to the police, others in districts with a low general rate of delinquency, practically all who have adolescent boys, however, producing young delinquents. These families were shown to have little in common with one another: some of the fathers are hard-working, others permanently unemployed; some are mentally or physically sick, others of good general health. Some of the mothers are quite capable of running a house, others don't know how to cook. Some of the families live in old, dilapidated houses, others in roomy quarters on an estate. Although the income of most of the families are low, they vary from an irregular unskilled worker's wage to that of a semi-skilled steel erector. Although in essence these families have little, if anything, in common, the criterion for including them in the survey was that of inadequacy of performance. It was demonstrated that in a number of activities concerning health and hygiene, solvency and planning, and the children's education, these families fell short of the standards that the wider community has accepted as the compulsory minimum.

If, as was found in the last chapter, all these families produce a rate of juvenile delinquency that is double that of their immediate neighbours in districts with a high rate of delinquency, and eight times that for the general population of the city, it appears that the explanation of this phenomenon lies in the way of living of these families. Different though the personalities are that make up the fifty-two families, their patterns of living are very similar. There are two main factors that dominate the children's lives. These can be found in all the families for long periods, and in many of them persistently. They are (i) poverty, and (ii) weak relationships with their parents and other adults.

(B) *Poverty*

It was shown in Chapter III that many of the families live permanently or for long periods on an income which is below subsistence level, taking as the standard the scale of the National Assistance Board. Other families have slightly higher incomes, but it was found that a small number of fathers (and one or two mothers) spent part of their incomes for personal purposes, thereby depriving their families of essential resources. The effect on the children in both groups is the same: they go short of essentials. There is not enough money to feed and clothe the children adequately, and to meet other needs. Their homes are inadequately furnished. When there is illness in the families no proper provisions for nursing the patient are made, nor, for that matter, could easily be made. A child that shares a bed with three or four sibs, and sometimes his parents, too—a bed made up more often of rags and old coats than of blankets, and very rarely covered with sheets—will not find much rest and comfort there. The provision of food is inadequate and irregular: a large meal may be provided when there is money in the house, and bread, baked beans, and tea may be all for the rest of the week. Often the child is prevented from attending school because clothes, or shoes, or food for breakfast, or dinner money are not there when needed. Poverty makes its mark on the child's life in many ways.

(C) *Parental guidance and handling of the children*

The second important factor appears to be the emotional insecurity experienced by the children in the relationship with their parents, primarily with their mothers. There is a good deal of sociological evidence, details of which will be given below, of the fact that the mother is not always and as a matter of certainty available to the child when the child needs her. Such unavailability may be due to a variety of reasons. One of them may be found in the character of the mother: the woman who cannot form a close relationship with her children, the psycho-pathic or 'affectionless' type (Bowlby, 1949). It may be due, on the other hand, to emotional immaturity of the parent: the mother may be so preoccupied with her own emotional prob-lems that she is not able to meet the needs of her children. It may, however, be simply due to the fact that the mother is mentally very retarded and unable to understand the demands made upon her by her children. Finally, and this is a factor that is at work to a greater or a less degree in all the families investi-gated, it may be apathy created in the mother by frequent preg-nancies, overwork, bad health, and constant money worries. Very often, it may be nothing but inability to cope with the demands of six or seven small children simultaneously. What-ever in psychiatric terms the explanation of the evidence offered below, it appears that the experience of uncertainty concerning mother is common among the children growing up under the conditions described on these pages. The picture that emerges may be summed up like this: 'Father and/or mother cannot always be depended on'. The mother appears to take no interest in the children, and sometimes she actually neglects them, although at the same time she may have affection for them or at least for some of them. The children in this setting of extreme material shortages which is not buffered by the parents' caring presence grow up in a very chill wind.

A good deal of the evidence on which the above suggestions are based has already appeared in previous pages. In particular the descriptions of family life contained in Chapter VI bear out the inability of the mothers to cope with all the demands of their children. It was, furthermore, one of the aims of the investigation to collect such information on a systematic basis. The questionnaire designed for health visitors and social workers contained a set of questions, some standardized and some open, concerning relationships between the parents and children of the research set. It was hoped to get answers from at least two independent workers for each family. The questionnaire, which is fully reproduced in Appendix II, was shaped on that used by S. and E. Glueck (1950). One of the questions concerned the cohesiveness of family life, and the answers offered were 'cohesive', or 'some elements of cohesion', or 'unintegrated'. The open questions concerned the supervision of the children by the father, and the affection given by each parent to each of the children. Although the questions should have been asked separately for each child in the family, it was soon apparent that such a task could not be carried out. Neither the health visitors nor the few social workers available for the interviews were sufficiently familiar with the families to be able spontaneously to answer these questions, by giving a detailed description of the parents' relationship with each child. In fact, even after discarding the original aim and lumping the questions together for a general account of intrafamiliar relationships, the picture obtained was very often a rather hazy one. It was obvious that such a task could not be carried out with the means available during this investigation, and that for eliciting information about intrafamilial relationships the skills of a psychiatric social worker would have to be used.

The health visitors and social workers have, however, given a general picture of the families known to them. This, with some exceptions, bears out the impressions gained by me during the personal interview and in the course of collecting information from other sources. The general atmosphere is haphazard; the father usually shows very little active interest, and, if he does, it is erratic. He may shout at or hit the children when they get in his way. In many cases the father was not personally known to the health visitor. The mother may try to supervise the children in her own way, to the best of her ability, but usually the remark was made that she might be more successful if she had fewer children, or if she had greater ability. In many cases the health visitor thinks that the mother does not supervise at all, and the children just 'run wild'. A few comments are quoted as illustrations. (The case numbers are those quoted in the tables in the appendix.)

Case 2.   Health visitor: The family is cohesive. I don't know about father's role. Mother lets the children run wild. She has affection for them. She just has no idea how to manage.

Social worker: Cohesive family. Father seems to exercise discipline, mother often says 'Wait till father comes home'. Her supervision not very effective, but she tries. Too many children. Has affection, definitely.

Case 3. Health visitor: Cohesive family. Very little discipline. No supervision by mother—Pat (eldest girl, aged ten) runs the family. There is affection, mother is quite happy, thinks she does well.

Social worker: Cohesive. Father exercises discipline, the children are rather afraid of him . . . She tries to the best of her ability. Both show affection.

Case 42. Health visitor: Some elements of cohesion in this family, a borderline case. No discipline exercised by father, the children are rather undisciplined. Mother does not bother about them, bad school attenders, sometimes months at a time. The parents go out at night. Not much affection there, most unpleasant type of people. Mother lies, dresses up and goes out, leaves children alone.

Case 4. Health visitor: Father shouts at the children, he is not without interest in them, the children fear him rather. Not much supervision by mother. She would shout at Margery (a mentally defective girl), is inclined to drive her instead of leading her. Difficult to say about affection.

Social worker: Some element of cohesion in this family. Considerable shouting by father, but to little effect. Totally inadequate supervision by mother. Father displays a good deal of affection, mother quite fond of them in her own way.

Case 51. Health visitor: This is an unintegrated family. Father dead. Mother does not supervise the children, and has never shown affection for them. The children haven't much chance, she shouts at them and pushes them out.

Case 20. Health visitor: Unintegrated family. Pam and Margaret are terrified of their step-mother. They are attached to the father, but he is not in the picture, works nights and sleeps all day. No supervision by the mother. The father has affection, but not the mother, they are unwanted children.

Case 22. Health visitor: Some element of cohesion. Father lax. Mother's supervision unsuitable, affection erratic, at times appears warm.

Social worker: Very little discipline there, father is lax, mother's supervision erratic, but they have affection for the children.

Case 33. Health visitor: Unintegrated family. No adequate supervision by mother, she just moans about them. I don't know about the father. Mother has affection in a soft way . . . she worries, but doesn't do anything. She won't work, a shiftless, soft creature.

Second health visitor: Unintegrated family. Mother is afraid of having the children taken from her, but she is far too soft with them, complains about them in front of them, is not respected by them. She easily lets herself go, maybe the weight of everything is getting her down.

Case 41. Health visitor: Cohesive family. Can't say about father. Mother shouts and swears at children. She shows affection for baby. A rough lot all of them.

Second health visitor: Cohesive family. Stick together. Father is indifferent to the children. Mother shouts at them, not much supervision. Affectionate with the baby.

Case 47. Health visitor: A cohesive family, but not much discipline exercised by father. Mother does not supervise properly, she is very lazy, but she may feel poorly. There is affection . . . If she can stop having children she might improve, it is all on top of her.

From the above quotations—taken at random from different types of families—it can be seen that there is a lack of guidance, or coherence, in handling the children. This may be due to the mother's lack of interest in them, or due to her inability to run a large family, but, whatever the reason, the method of handling the children is much the same in most families. These findings are very similar to the observations made by Andry (1960) in an investigation of boys from a delinquency area in London. He confined his study to boys who came from unbroken working-class homes and did not show symptoms of neurosis or psychopathy. The samples consisted of recidivist thieves from a remand home, and they were compared to non-delinquent controls from two secondary modern schools. Andry's observations are based on the children's perception of the roles played by their parents, and on interviews with the parents. He found that the fathers of delinquents tended to have less leisure time available for contacts with their children than did fathers of non-delinquent controls. There was less father-child sharing of hobbies and outings. It is interesting to note that the delinquent boys (aged between twelve and fifteen) were troubled by their fathers' defective roles. When in trouble, the bulk of delinquents tended not to contact their parents, whereas the bulk of non-delinquent controls did. The fathers of delinquents did not appear clearly as the effective leaders of the family, were not as 'reasonable' in meting out punishment, did not strike a balance as regards strictness, and did not praise as consistently as the fathers of non-delinquent controls. In all the differences that emerged between delinquents and controls it was the in-adequacy of the fathers' roles rather than the mothers' roles which differentiated the two groups.

(D) *Affection and family cohesion*
The erratic ways of handling the children are in no way con-nected with the absence of affection. In fact, in the majority of cases the presence of affection was commented on. This may explain the curious fact that most of the children of the re-search set are described by their teachers as normal well-adjusted children who display few, if any, nervous symptoms. This fact is also commented on by Hilda Lewis (1954), who says that the proportion of children undisturbed in behaviour is considerably higher in 'problem' families than in the general run of children admitted to the reception centre of a children's department. The cohesiveness of the family, the feeling of belonging together of brothers and sisters, is perhaps an even stronger element than the haphazard demonstration of affection by the parents, which is in any case not always present. One of the comments made frequently by those who knew the families was that there was a strong feeling of loyalty between brothers and sisters. It is very likely that this experience of being one of a group of sibs, who all share alike in the ups and downs of life, strengthens the individual child and makes him more able to face his daily trials.

There was, on the other hand, a set of children who did show signs of emotional disturbance. There are six families whose eldest children are the offspring of previous unions of either the mother or the father. They are, therefore, only half-sibs of the younger children, and apparently they are not fully accepted by the younger sibs. The following case records have been collected.

Case 19. Richard, only son of father's previous marriage, mother dead, eldest child in present family.

Probation officer: Richard is a quiet and inoffensive type of boy, who states that he does not go to school because 'he does not like it'. He is enuretic. There appears to be some domestic trouble between the parents and there is very little parental guidance. The boy has lacked control and advice at home.

Case 20. Pam and Margaret, daughters of father's previous marriage, mother dead, eldest children in present family.

Probation officer: It seems that Pam and Margaret are not treated as well as the mother's own children—she told me that Pam often and Margaret very occasionally wet the bed and she hit them sharply on the legs for this and they have not done it since. She feels that it is due entirely to laziness . . . Margaret's and Pam's form teachers remarked on the astonishing difference in them while they were at the children's home. Not only were they cleaner and tidier in appearance but they seemed happier and more contented too.

Health visitor: Pam reported to be frequently thrown out by stepmother, crying bitterly. The stepmother's language is foul.

Case 24. Charles, illegitimate son of mother, eldest of present family.

Consulting psychiatrist, Child Guidance Clinic: Charles gave a very poor account of himself, and his replies to all personal questions were either monosyllabic or 'I don't know' . . . Any subjects broached which did not touch upon his personal or family life were discussed with complete freedom and vivacity. . . . He has no real interests, and from his story one gets the feeling that he is a rather lonely little boy . . . When questions are asked about his stepfather he becomes quite mute and sullen. When questioned why he sleeps out in hedges at night at times he can give no reason. When questioned about whether he is happy at home and his home life, one again gets only the response, 'I don't know'. During the course of the interview one arrives at the conclusion that he has no particular affection for his parents or family and has no real happiness in his home environment; for example it slips out that he is happier in the remand home and would not mind staying there altogether.

Case 26. Jean, eldest child of mother's previous marriage, father dead, eldest of present family, various delinquencies.
Approved school report: The letters from home have been few . . . The stepfather would not have her in the house. I think it would be advisable for her to have Christmas here.
Second approved school report: Jean has received no letters from her people for a very long time, and about two months ago her weekly letter home was returned marked 'Gone away'.
Peter, second child of mother's previous marriage, father dead.
Child Guidance Clinic: The mother neglects the older children for those of the second marriage. The stepfather is not very kind to Peter. Peter had impetigo of scalp, clothes dirty and smelly . . . The stealing episode resulted from him being given several pounds to pay a grocery bill from which he took 10s od. He also admitted stealing foodstuffs at home.

Case 27. Allan, illegitimate son of mother, eldest child in present family.
Probation officer: Allan broke into a shop near his home. Apparently his mother sent him to buy a loaf of bread, but he left it too late till the shops were closed. Thinking that he would be severely chastised if he returned empty-handed, he broke into the shop. Stepfather does not seem to have much affection for Allan. Both mother and Allan seem frightened of him.
Approved school report: Allan is a very maladjusted and deeply disturbed boy and this . . . gives rise to strong anti-social tendencies . . . no moral values whatsoever.

Case 32. Robert, illegitimate son of mother, eldest of present family.
Child Guidance Clinic: He informed me that he is not happy at home, that he does not get enough food and he gets no pocket money.

In all these cases it appears that there is tension between step-parent and children, and that there are signs of emotional disturbance. Three of the children had been referred to the Child Guidance Clinic.

(E) *Links with the wider family*
Although it is likely that the children derive much emotional

comfort from each other (excepting the above-mentioned half-sibs), it appears that they have very little opportunity of making a relationship with grandparents, uncles, aunts and cousins. Most of the research families had no or only very loose connections with their wider kin. In the course of the interview that I had with the mothers and sometimes the fathers the question was asked whether any relatives were available when needed to give a hand in the house, as for instance during the mother's confinements, or illnesses. In four cases, belonging to the pilot survey, this question had not been included in the questionnaire. In a further ten cases the topic was not discussed, either because the mother appeared unreliable in what she had said so far, or because there was not sufficient rapport. But out of thirty-eight families where this question was discussed, there were only six in which there was a link of some sort with the wider family:

(i) Family 51 was sharing house with the maternal grandmother.

(ii) Family 4 had a loose link with the maternal grandmother, who took over in cases of crises, as for instance for a short period when the mother was in a mental hospital. She also took in one of her granddaughters for a short time after the girl had been put under the supervision of a probation officer for non-attendance at school. But this relationship was of a rough nature, both grandmother and mother cursing each other freely in court and in front of social workers. It seemed that the grandmother still felt obliged to assist the family although she did not approve of the daughter's way of living. The grandmother was described as an 'old-fashioned, very respectable type of working woman' by the child care officer.

(iii) The mother of family 7 frequently spent the day at her mother's house. In this family the marriage was very unstable.

(iv) In family 13 the maternal grandmother came every Monday to give a hand. They lived near each other.

(v) A similar arrangement existed in family 42. This grandmother sometimes had one of the children staying with her.

(vi) In family 44 the paternal grandmother, another 'hardworking old woman, simple, straightforward, old-fashioned' (child care officer), tried to keep the family going. She went shopping for them regularly and visited once a week. One granddaughter, who had a fit person order, was fostered with this grandmother.

In the great majority of cases, however, such links with kin did not exist. In many families I was told that their relations lived too far away to be visited. Whether there were also tensions and quarrels could not always be ascertained. The answer of ten mothers was that their people lived too far away to be visited. In seventeen further families there were hints of a break. For instance, family 23 had two sons removed under fit person orders who were then fostered out with their maternal grandmother, and 'she won't have anything to do with her daughter' (child care officer). The mother of family 28 talked about a sister 'up the valleys, but I don't bother with her, she don't approve of Mr ——' (her husband). Her husband, she said, had a brother in another part of Seaport, but they never saw him, they had a row after their father's death. Another mother, of family 45, said that her mother had married again and was living in Seaport, but they had found that in case of need friends would come in, indicating that she did not get on with her stepfather. The mother of family 22 answered, 'I don't bother with relations on either side'. The mother of family 49 indicated that she could not visit her mother because her mother did not approve of the man she was living with. One mother just said that they were a large family but 'I don't see them much'. There were two mothers who said that their own people were dead and they 'did not bother' with their husbands' people. In addition to these there were five families whose mothers had been brought up in children's homes or by foster parents, and they all stated that they had no relations (Cases 20, 24, 43, 16, and 38).

The general impression was one of almost complete severance of links with the wider kin, with the exception of the six cases described above. When I asked the mothers about 'their people' they usually meant this to refer to their own relations, and they usually mentioned their husbands' kin only on further promptings. That the links with kin are very loose was confirmed by health visitors who were well aware of the absence of relatives during critical periods, such as confinements or illnesses of the mother. The importance of this gap in the social network of the research families must not be underrated. Recent community studies in London (Young and Willmott, 1957; and Bott, 1957) have emphasized the importance of family-connectedness in working-class households. The Bethnal Green study of Young and Willmott describes the 'great triangle' of family life—mum, wife and husband. Bott points out that close ties with the wider family are frequently in existence in working-class households, and where they are fractured through removal to another district, for instance, or through death, they are usually counterbalanced by a closer partnership between husband and wife. This, however, necessitates a new orientation concerning the sources to which the family turn for reference in value judgements. In the close-knit kinship group ideas and opinions are shaped and re-shaped in constant group-intercommunication, and deviation from group opinions is rapidly corrected by such mechanisms as gossip, cold-shouldering, ridicule, ostracism or straight criticism. Where close-knit kinship ties are non-existent, the family has to form its own standards and turn to 'ideas' for reference; and modern mass-media increasingly supply such ideas ranging from simple housekeeping hints to complex relationship problems. The importance of intelligence and a basic education to fit the family to such a living pattern is immediately obvious. The research families were on the whole handicapped in this respect, and an absence of the supporting kinship group could therefore not be counterbalanced by the development of an internalized value system. The essential framework for consistent behaviour training of the children was non-existent. Furthermore, the children lacked opportunities for forming a warm relationship with an adult other than their parents, who would show a personal interest in them and who would be available for guidance or support if this was needed.

(F) *Marital relationships*

Within the framework of the present investigation it was not possible to assess husband-wife relationships in psychiatric terms. Two sociological observations, however, were undertaken, the value of which is doubtful. One was in the form of questions to health visitors and social workers, the results of which will be discussed further on. The other was a search of the matrimonial court records for evidence of separations or other court orders made for the maintenance of the family. (For a detailed tabulation see Appendix X.)

Thirty-five families showed no evidence of previous separations or divorces. There was one family headed by a mother who had divorced her husband. Four families had one spouse previously married and divorced. In six families a legal separation had been obtained once, but had lapsed. In one family a legal separation had been obtained twice, but had lapsed. In one family a legal separation had been obtained three times, but had lapsed on all three occasions. There were two families living as husband and wife who were not married. In two families one of the partners was dead.

If to this information is added the information gleaned from files and interviews, the following picture emerges: At the time of the investigation all eight couples who had obtained separation orders were living together again. Since then, however, two other couples have obtained such orders. It appears that these arrangements are usually not very long lasting. The following statement was made by a member of the public health department:

Mother states that she has been legally separated from father for six months, although he still lives in the same house and she still prepares his meals, as she says he will beat her if she does not.

In addition to the families with legal separations there are two in which the father deserted the family for lengthy periods, but returned eventually. In another case the mother left her family of six children and went to London but she returned six weeks later. In three further cases the father was known to have an association with another woman. In one of these the affair came to an end after about two years, after which there was an immediate improvement in the mother's housekeeping, as she had more money. The father had been seriously ill, was nursed by his wife, and then broke off the former relationship. In another family the woman with whom the father associated died, after giving birth to four children. This man also raised a family of six children with his wife at the same time. In the third family at the time of the investigation the father was still associating with the other woman, and he had two illegitimate children for whom there were affiliation orders. His wife seemed more concerned about the drain on their income than the moral aspects of this association. There were three further families whose mothers were known to have extra-marital relations. One mother usually had a man in the house, referred to as 'uncle' by her children, when the husband was in prison. Another mother had a 'boy friend' as he was referred to; her husband, a permanently unemployed man, had become prematurely senile. A third mother had had two illegitimate children who were conceived while her husband was in prison. This makes a total of nine families with irregularities in their marital relations. If to this group of nine is added the group of eight who at one time or another had legal separations, one divorced mother, and two families unmarried who are bringing up children of previous unions together with their joint children, this makes a total of twenty families known to have some instabilities in their marital relations. It cannot from this be concluded that all the remaining thirty families with both parents living have stable marital relations.

The second line of enquiry was a standardized set of questions to health visitors and social workers. Marital relationships were to be assessed as either normal, or as containing friction, or indifference. These assessments were made for forty-four families, since five families were not visited by health visitors or social workers, two parents were widowed, and one parent was divorced. In twenty-one cases a social worker's as well as a health visitor's assessment was obtained; they agreed in nine cases and differed in twelve. It is difficult to sum up because of this large number of discrepant assessments. Perhaps the only conclusion one can draw was that there were four families described as having normal relationships by both health visitors and social workers, with no evidence from the court to contradict this, plus another nine families known only to health visitors, who described them as normal, with again no contradictory evidence from elsewhere. This makes a total of thirteen families. The remaining seventeen families could not be gauged.

There was a good deal of evidence of aggressiveness and physical violence among the twenty families about whom we collected information in the courts. Here are some examples:

(i) Health visitor: Mother had been to hospital with concussion. Father hit her.

(ii) Health visitor: Father had been quarrelling with mother a lot—finally he knocked her front teeth out.

Housing Department: I met his wife who had a plaster on her forehead owing to [the father] hitting her necessitating three stitches in her head.

Housing Department: Next door neighbour was interviewed and corroborated statement of drunkenness, banging doors, swearing, dragging wife downstairs and screaming.

(iii) Housing Department: Mother asked for transfer owing to behaviour of father who is continually drunk and causes frequent scenes in the house with consequent complaints from neighbours.

Co-ordination Committee: Mother sent to police to have father forcibly removed.

(iv) NSPCC: Mother complained of father maltreating her because he didn't have an interesting supper.

(v) Probation officer: Mother had plenty of evidence that father is still carrying on with the girl . . . and they had a real row, mother breaking the plaster of her fractured arm when she hit him with it.

Housing Department: Neighbours are frequently disturbed by father and mother quarrelling. At a recent inspection mother was suffering from fractured ribs alleged to have been done when she was attacked by father.

(vi) Co-ordination Committee: Main difficulty: incompatibility of parents. Father deserted mother nine times . . . Father and mother reconciled several times, but as soon as mother is pregnant father leaves her.

(vii) Police constable: . . . father was well known to the police, and father and mother were becoming a serious problem in the district. Apparently it is their habit to go out at night leaving their three children (all under eight) alone in the house. They return about 10.45 the worse for drink. Fighting commences, language is foul, and on numerous occasions the police have been called out. Not once but many times father and mother have chased each other up and down the street.

2. AN INTERPRETATION

The main features concerning the children's upbringing which have been found to exist in these families appear to be:

(i) mothers who exercise little, if any, supervision,

(ii) fathers whose handling of the children is either lax or erratic,

(iii) close loyalty between sibs, and

(iv) no links or only loose links with the wider family.

Relations between father and mother were found to vary from extremely unstable to apparently normal, with a large middle section about whom little could be ascertained. The degree of affection of the parents for the children appeared to vary, too, from a very warm relationship to the cold atmosphere engendered by a mother who appeared to be a psychopathic character. What kind of experiences is a child likely to have in an environment containing these features?

The infant is born into a setting where his physical needs are rarely, if ever, fully met. In addition to the normal discomforts of a stage at which dependency needs are greatest, the infant has to struggle with inadequate and irregular feeding, with unsuitable clothing and bed-clothing, and with skin irritations caused by insufficient cleanliness. There are records of children who had to be admitted to hospital for treatment of sore buttocks. One infant, admitted to hospital, had the pattern of a wire mattress imprinted on his back. There are references by health visitors to the fact that the mothers kept their babies indoors all day with the windows shut.

The infant's early emotional experiences of being alive are closely linked with his physical well-being, and in this process he gradually forms a relationship with his mother. He experiences her love for him, the attention she gives him, the amount of care he receives. The infant in an environment like that described in these pages will not have his early needs fully satisfied; he will experience continuous or frequent frustrations. He will learn at an early stage that there are not many people around him who can be depended upon for the satisfaction of his needs.

Furthermore, it appears that in the families described the important early training period is missed out in which the child begins to understand the demands of society in the form of the parents' picture of the 'acceptable child' (Josselyn, 1948). There is no systematic toilet training, there is no insistence on manners, there is no conformity by the parents themselves to a code of manners. There are no generally accepted standards in the erratic, unplanned, day-to-day way of living. The parents may quarrel with each other, and, if they do, will do so in front of the children. The child will not get a chance to experience the gratification obtained by conforming with the parents' wishes. He will not be praised for some small feat of self-discipline. His first encounter with demands for self-discipline and adherence to rules is likely to be at school. The impact of such demands will be so much the heavier because he has not gone through the normal preparatory stages. School routine, with its requirements concerning polite manners, cleanliness, obedience, concentration, and postponement of immediate desires, is likely to be very difficult to accept, and this difficulty is bound to affect the learning process. It often results in absenteeism. Once the habit of truanting is formed it is difficult to break it, and the parents are not likely to assist the child in getting rid of such a habit. Under such conditions a child is unable to form a close relationship with his teacher, in which he could turn the teacher into a parent-figure, a loved and respected person from whom he could accept demands. The second chance for the child to respond to the demands of society is missed. The period at which a child is normally ready to understand and internalize such demands, the period of super-ego formation, is wasted.

It is difficult to draw a picture of such experiences in general terms without falling into the error of over-simplification, or of leaving unmentioned the incidents that do not happen to fall into the pattern. If such an attempt is made, it is done in constant awareness of the fact that such a picture is meant only to serve as a suggestion of prevailing conditions.

There appears to be ample evidence that these children have indeed no super-ego, no conception of what is right and wrong.

The following excerpts from various files are examples of observations made about some of the children:

Case 8. School report to Child Guidance Clinic. It would appear that she lacks ability to distinguish between right and wrong as measured by conventional standards.

Case 9. Probation officer. Donald has no sense of right and wrong, he is fearless. He leads other boys into mischief.

Superintendent of remand home: Donald's conceptions of right and wrong are extremely hazy, and he would very easily follow other boys into any reckless offence. It appears that parental control must be extremely lax.

Case 51. Probation officer: James appears to have no sense of guilt but feels it is his right to have money for the cinema. He goes every night . . . James' creed is now, 'I see, I want, I take'. If he remains in this environment there is little one can do.

Case 16. Superintendent of remand home: Philip is an unenterprising, weak-willed boy of negative personality and little strength of character. He has few scruples concerning right and wrong behaviour and would probably easily yield to further foolish irresponsible conduct.

Case 19. Probation officer: There is very little parental guidance. The boy has lacked control and advice at home . . . Both parents are weak and apathetic.

Superintendent of remand home: His sense of responsibility is poor . . . complete disregard for the truth. He appears to have had very little parental guidance, he is wild and untrained.

Case 22. Probation officer: Robert is very out of hand. He thinks nothing of mitching and takes no notice of punishment. Doesn't care two hoots.

Case 27. Superintendent of remand home: Allan is a negative weak-charactered boy possessing very little sense of responsibility, who needs proper supervision and guidance.

Headmaster of approved school: Allan . . . a deeply disturbed boy . . . no moral values whatsoever.

Case 28. Head teacher: These children have no sense of right and wrong. They will take anything at school.

Case 32. Child Guidance Clinic: Norman is undoubtedly easily led and lacks the ability to appreciate the real significance of his misdoings. In this case . . . there is a complete lack of parental guidance and control.

Case 48. Probation officer: Stephen does not appreciate that he has done anything wrong. He told me the story as an adventure. There is no real harm in Stephen, but he is unused to discipline and just does what he feels like.

Superintendent of remand school: Paul (Stephen's brother) often shows a good sense of humour and at his best he is a pleasant, bright, happy, very likeable youngster. Against this . . . his character is still weak and undeveloped, he is often wild and irresponsible, he easily yields to temptation. Scruples and the morals of honesty mean very little to him.

3. PARENTAL CRIMINAL RECORDS

If the above suggestions concerning the children's character formation are valid interpretations of the high delinquency rate, then they should not need any further explanation in terms of parental anti-social conduct. That the children were not encouraged to adopt normal behaviour patterns seemed clear; it was of some interest, however, to find out whether they were actively encouraged to commit anti-social acts. Did the parents know what their children were doing, and did they condone their activities? Such attitudes are difficult, if not impossible, to ascertain; indirectly, however, a certain amount of information came to light. In some cases there were notes by officials pointing out that not the children, but their parents were ultimately to blame for their delinquencies:

Case 1. Police officer: I received no assistance from the parents . . .

Case 4. Child Guidance Clinic: It is significant that the child is kept home from school and encouraged in various other minor anti-social behaviour by her mother, who makes all excuses, mostly lies, to account for her non-attendance.

Case 24. Probation officer: The boy himself presents little cause for anxiety . . . clearly not a boy-problem but a parent-problem. The trouble and difficulty seems undoubtedly to rest with the irresponsibility of the parents, not with the boy.

Case 26. Health visitor: Peter's behaviour was only in keeping with the standards of his home.

I came across two cases where parent and child were convicted together. In one, the mother and daughter were caught shoplifting. In the other mother and son jointly stole a registered postal packet. But in many other cases I got the impression that the mother at least was unaware of the children's activities, and quite incapable of handling them. For instance, in case 27, a probation officer says: 'Mother a dull weak personality, indolent and apathetic, incapable of providing the moral guidance which the children need'. The same view is expressed by Andry who says that the deviant behaviour of delinquent boys he interviewed in London was on the whole little known to their parents.

Apart from the parents' knowledge of their children's delinquencies, we asked ourselves, were they themselves delinquent, or had they been at an earlier age? If there was a criminal tradition in the family it was likely to be adopted by the children. A search of the police records gave the following results: in twenty families neither parent had any criminal conviction. In a further twenty families the father had been convicted of at least one indictable offence, and in a further five families the mother had been convicted of one or more indictable offences. There were another two families where both parents had such convictions. There were five families where either the father or the mother or both had convictions for child neglect only. Since in a good many cases child neglect arises out of unintended consequences of certain actions by the parents which they had not foreseen, for purposes of this enquiry a conviction for child neglect only without any further convictions was not used as an index for inclusion in the group of convicted parents. Altogether there were ten families with such convictions, five of them had no other convictions, the other five appear in the group who had other convictions. (See Appendix XI.)

Most of the offences committed by the fathers were larcenies, very often connected with breaking and entering. All twenty-two fathers with convictions other than child neglect had at least one for larceny. Nine fathers had in addition convictions for burglary or breaking and entering. The next largest group was that convicted of wilful or malicious damage, assault, and unlawful or malicious wounding, involving fourteen men. Two men had indecently assaulted young girls. Five men had convictions for false pretences. A full list appears in Appendix XII.

There were seven mothers who had convictions other than for child neglect. One of them is mentally ill, and she had a record of malicious wounding, assault, and wilful damage. She has been a mental hospital in-patient on several occasions. Four women had convictions for false pretences, two of them also for larcenies. Two women had been convicted of larcenies only, mainly shoplifting.

We asked ourselves whether the twenty-seven families with criminal records produced more delinquent children than the twenty with no records. (For reasons given above, the five parents convicted of child neglect only were excluded from this test.)

A comparison of the two groups showed that there was a negative correlation between convictions of parents and children. (For details see Appendix XIII.) Taking boys aged 8-13, we found that those of convicted parents produced a delinquency rate of thirty-eight per hundred boys at risk; whereas the boys from non-criminal parents produced a rate of forty-seven per hundred at risk. The contrast was more startling for boys in the 14-17-year-old group. The boys of convicted parents had a delinquency rate of fifty-five per hundred boys at risk, whereas the boys from non-criminal parents had a rate of ninety-three per hundred at risk. Generally speaking and taking the two age groups together we found that well under half of the boys of criminal parents were themselves delinquent, whereas two-thirds of the boys with non-criminal parents were delinquent. (The difference is significant at the five per cent level. Chi-squared equals 4.6 with one degree of freedom.)

For the girls the difference was in the same direction, but it was not as great as for the boys. In the age group 8-13, the girls of convicted parents produced a delinquency rate of eight per hundred girls at risk, whereas for girls of non-criminal parents the rate was thirty. In the age group 14-17 the girls' delinquency rate was sixty-seven per hundred at risk for convicted parents, and forty-two for non-criminal parents. Here the pattern did not repeat, but on taking the age groups together we found that only one-fifth of the girls of convicted parents were delinquent, but one-third of the girls belonging to non-criminal parents were delinquent. (The difference does not reach statistical significance. Chi-squared equals 1.6.) It is obvious, however, that criminality of the parents does not increase the likelihood of children being convicted of juvenile delinquency. The reason for the negative correlation is not clear. (A member of the police force suggested the reason was obvious: the children of criminal parents are more skilled at the job, and more skilled at denying their gilt when caught!) The fact, however, that the children of non-criminal parents were even more delinquent than the others proved that their delinquencies arise out of living conditions in general rather than parental precept.

4. MATERNAL DEPRIVATION THROUGH SEPARATION

There was another aspect that might have an effect on delinquent character formation, and that is the concept elaborated by Bowlby (1944), who in comparing a group of juvenile thieves with a control group of maladjusted children demonstrated that prolonged mother-child separation in the first five years bears an aetiological relationship to a certain form of persistent stealing. In later work Bowlby (1956) somewhat modified his earlier concepts and he concluded that 'Statements implying that children who are brought up in institutions or who suffer other forms of serious privation or deprivation in early life commonly develop psychopathic or affectionless characters are seen to be mistaken'. In 1958 he sums up his views by stating: 'Although the study showed that there was much variation of outcome, it did nothing to cast doubt on the many studies which indicate that some children in their personality development suffer grave damage and others lesser damage from a separation experience; nor did it detract in any way from the studies . . . which confirm the common observation that during a separation experience and after return home a majority of young children are emotionally disturbed . . .'

While, therefore, it appears that prolonged separation from the mother before the age of five need not affect the ability to make warm and lasting friendships and to have a normal personality development, it may do so in certain cases. It was important, therefore, to investigate the incidence of maternal separation which might have an effect on the high delinquency rate in our research families. The results were negative: only one boy had a period in a children's home when under five. He was admitted aged two when his parents lived in a basement room. He re-joined them aged five when they were rehoused. He appeared in the juvenile court for the first time aged eight. Two of his brothers, who also became delinquent, had remained with their parents. None of the delinquent children had any records of lengthy stays in hospitals or convalescent homes.

Here again it is interesting to compare these results with observations made by Andry in a study of delinquent boys in London. He stresses the point that the mother's role in the child's character formation has been overemphasized at the cost of the importance of the father's role. He cannot find a significant difference between delinquents and non-delinquent controls concerning separation from their mothers during early childhood.

Since neither a criminal tradition nor maternal deprivation had any specific bearing on the rate of delinquency produced by the research families, it appears that the mere fact of child neglect was the primary causative factor.

CHAPTER IX

CONCLUSIONS

THE survey described on the preceding pages, although small in scale, will help us to answer some of the questions posed in the introductory chapters. We have seen that juvenile delinquency is generated in the type of family that often comes to the notice of the local authority because of suspected child neglect. Neither the geographical location nor the personalities of the parents affect this process; and it appears that this type of delinquency is the behaviour pattern of a child who by trial and error has learnt to cope with various life situations unconscious of the moral demands made by society. Neither his parents nor the wider family have taken an active part in his upbringing, and his teachers have not been able to form a constructive relationship with him because of his irregular attendance at school. He has learnt to avoid pain and to seek immediate pleasure, and in this daily battle under conditions which are often harsh he has found comfort in the presence of his brothers and sisters. This has helped him to develop a friendly, happy-go-lucky disposition; he feels accepted within his own large family. When he has been caught committing a delinquency he has shown complete unawareness of the moral nature of his act.

The delinquencies he commits are not behaviour patterns instilled into him by his elders; they are the only method by which he can get what he wants, a method learnt in infancy. He has no belongings of his own, even his clothes are second-hand, passed on, and often shared with sibs. He takes what he needs and does not understand that such an act may be 'wrong'. He has no guilt feelings, but fear of punishment, of being caught, may eventually teach him to be more careful when he takes what he thinks he needs. He may live in a district where lorry-skipping and shoplifting expeditions on a Saturday morning to Woolworth's are part of the game of living, and he may join in this. But his behaviour pattern was shaped at a much earlier stage, and he will pinch and snatch whether or not his neighbourhood frowns upon it.

This type of delinquency which is born out of neglect is different in nature from delinquency arising in a home that is well aware of the moral standards of society. The neglected child is ignorant of what he ought to do; the other child is delinquent in spite of what he knows he ought to do. There is no similarity in the act, and treatment must of necessity be different. If this is true, it follows that future delinquency research must learn to differentiate between such different activities as 'neglect-delinquency', 'environmental delinquescent behaviour', 'guilt-delinquency', and so on. It may then be possible to find out which type of delinquency is most frequently linked with recidivism; which type of delinquency is most likely to develop into adult criminality, and possibly also into which type of adult criminality. Furthermore, it may become possible by differentiating between the various types of delinquents to understand the peculiar rhythmic peak formations in our national crime statistics. The three-year wave patterns which occurred pretty uniformly in different police districts over the country between 1945 and 1954 and the steep rise in crime which followed them have an internal logic which so far has remained unexplained. It may be possible, by breaking up the crime statistics of a particular police district into different types of offenders as suggested above, and by following individual case records over a period of years to throw some light on the mysterious similarity of crime patterns in different localities. Is there, for instance, a fairly constant delinquent population which is of the type described on these pages? There are indications that in spite of minor fluctuations 'neglect-delinquency' is of a pretty constant character; the boys thieve a lot, but they appear in court only when the police happens to catch them. Is on the other hand the occasional peak of the crime curve made up by a different type of delinquent, the non-recidivist perhaps? These questions cannot be answered yet.

We can, however, say a little more about the parents of the young delinquents described above. It has been stressed before that the only characteristic the parents share is the very negative one of being unable to cope with the demands made upon them by the community. They cannot cope for many different reasons, and these range from mental defect, and other personality problems to such merely external factors as low income in large families. We have found that some of the parents have themselves a criminal record, and others have none; that marital relations in some families are normal, whereas in others there is a history of continuous tension. Indeed, it has been impossible to find a single characteristic shared by all. But since the total case load had been referred originally merely because of an inability to look after the children, this finding does not surprise us. What is more surprising, perhaps, is the fact that these people, heterogeneous though they are, all manage by their way of living to produce delinquent children. This phenomenon is one that must be seen as arising out of a specific home setting, and yet not closely linked with the personalities of the parents; unless the link is seen in a negative way: the parents all don't do what parents ought to do.

It is surprising, furthermore, that these families are so frequently dealt with as a homogeneous entity. The myth of the 'problem family' has lingered for many generations in the shape of Hogarth's Gin Alley population, the Wood Report's 'Social Problem Group', or the 'Co-ordination Committee Case-load' of the mid-twentieth century. Philp and Timms (1957) did much in their critical survey of the existing literature to explode the myth. The evidence offered on the preceding pages may help to give an understanding of the wide variety of factors that lead to a socially unacceptable way of living. It may also help to create a new approach to the problem of child neglect and to the problem of delinquency which arises out of it.

It is obvious that none of the inadequacies found among the research set of families is unique or specific to this particular group of people. Any of the indices of inadequacy mentioned in the literature concerned with the group can equally be found in other strata of society. The determining factor that brings to the notice of the local authority a family possessing any such indices of inadequacy is probably the fact that they lack the support of their own kin, that they cannot buy any help, and that the local authority is not in a position to give them the assistance they are in need of. This must not be interpreted as meaning that in those few cases where the inability to cope is directly linked with irresponsible behaviour, the blame lies with the community. The man who spends his weekly earnings in the pub is certainly responsible for this culpable action; but is it right to penalize his wife and children by not giving them the necessary support? A support, moreover, which she would probably find among her own relatives in the normal family setting. If she belonged to a higher-income group she would have financial resources to fall back on. In fact, it appears that a low income per head coupled with social isolation determine whether a family possessing certain characteristics (which are widely shared in the community) becomes a social nuisance. To substantiate this argument it is necessary to draw to some extent on the literature concerned with so-called 'problem families'.

One of the indices mentioned most frequently in the literature and which was most apparent in the Seaport research set is dirtiness. The causes of such a state are usually recognized to be manifold; they will range from the inherent incapacity of a mother to grasp the elements of hygiene and cleanliness to the apathy of an overworked, sick mother with a large family of young children. Neither instance could be considered a determinant in the making of a 'problem family'; in a higher income group an untidy woman could afford additional domestic help, and if she had a large family she would certainly do so. But when extra help cannot be afforded, it is normally the mother's mother who gives a hand, as has been shown in the Bethnal Green study by Young and Willmott (1957). Only in cases of severance of links with kin will the mother come to the notice of the health visitor if she cannot cope by herself.

Another factor which is usually mentioned in the literature is the very low general standard of living. There is no doubt that in this group subsistence needs cannot always be met. The reasons are again manifold. They may be, for instance, a low wage coupled with a large number of children; frequent ill-health of the wage earner; unemployment; or actual mis-spending by one or the other parent. It has been shown that the low income per head which exists in a number of the research families demands great skills in housecraft to satisfy all needs of the family. Similar considerations apply to the families who live on social payments during unemployment or sickness. Although they may suffice to tide over a family with some savings and a fairly adequately equipped household, they are hardly sufficient where this is not the case, and they become entirely inadequate when the family has to rely on such payments frequently or for lengthy periods. That this is so is borne out by an investigation of a large number of families on state-maintained incomes in Bristol (Shaw, 1958; Bowerbank, 1958). But beyond this, families whose previous income plus family allowances was below the rate they are entitled to under National Assistance Board regulations, will have a deduction made from their allowance so as to keep it in step with previous spending income. In effect many families have to live on incomes below subsistence level whether in or out of work. The families who cannot budget under such conditions can hardly be held responsible for their low standard of living. The problem of poverty caused by mis-spending will be discussed further down in conjunction with personality defects.

Child neglect, which receives much attention in the literature concerning these families, is closely linked with the general conditions of poverty. In fact, the definition of neglect is often given in terms of physical deprivation. The children are badly clothed, insufficiently cared for, and often badly nourished. If it is actually a lack of necessities, a higher income would put an end to this. But sometimes a mother appears to have an attitude of lack of interest in her children. This may be a frustration reaction born out of an insoluble financial problem. It may, on the other hand, be a psychopathic trait. In neither case can it be claimed that this factor as such is determinant in the making of child neglect, and will always lead to it. The affectionless character is not confined to one social stratum; and support from relatives, or a nannie, would prevent child neglect in a family setting of a higher income group. One of the factors contributing to the incidence of child neglect is the fact that these families have large numbers of children. Not only are limited economic resources overstrained, but also the mother's health suffers with continuous childbirth. What may appear as near-psychopathic carelessness to the observer may be nothing more than apathy and overtiredness. These children are neither planned nor really wanted once three or four are in the family. Birth control clinics provide an excellent service for women with a sufficiently high standard of living, but the methods advocated by them are quite unsuitable for mothers living under the conditions described on these pages.

Another aspect frequently mentioned in connection with the families referred to Co-ordination Committees is that of personality defects. The presence of traits loosely labelled psychopathic is mentioned in the literature, but there are no exact investigations and at present the term seems to be used as a convenient label for a personality that cannot be described in a more exact way. Psychopathy—whatever that may mean—is not confined to the lowest income groups, and can be coped with in higher income groups without heavy repercussions on the rest of the family. Statements are often made concerning intellectual or mental defects of persons belonging to the group under investigation, but these are not usually based on evidence. One of the few exact investigations of the intelligence of mothers convicted of child neglect was made by Sheridan (1956). With the exception of a small group of intelligent mothers the distribution of intelligence quotients followed a curve similar to the normal curve, but was displaced widely to the lower end of the scale, so that the average IQ was only 79.8. It is interesting to see that this is very close to the average obtained for children in the Seaport survey. In describing the personalities of the duller mothers Sheridan suggests apathy and lethargy which reminded her of the 'dazed inertia of severe physical or mental shock . . . possibly due to malnutrition or to the dulling effect of the repeated assault of adverse circumstance'. This fairly high incidence of dull and mentally retarded mothers is probably a contributing factor in many cases of extremely adverse circumstances, but there is no reason to believe that a low IQ by itself would make a mother an incompetent one. Early and efficient training will enable a woman in the fifty to seventy IQ range to carry out routine work without additional support. It is only in cases of unusual burdens, such as the rearing of a large family on a low income, or a series of crises without support, that breakdown is likely to occur sooner than with a mother of a higher intelligence who can use her resources more wisely. The vital causative factor here again appears to be the absence of the necessary supportive services, so that in the final analysis it is not a specific mental trait of the mother, but the inadequacy of the social services which in some cases allows such a handicap to result in living-conditions that the community is unable to tolerate.

Many reports mention 'character defects' which are alleged to play a role in the aetiology. Blacker (1952), for instance, mentions 'the frequent instability of the sexual lives previously led by the head of the house or the housewife'. But none of the instances mentioned by him, such as cohabiting, or having been married before, or even illegitimacy, are in evidence to a degree not found elsewhere. Premarital sexual relations are a widely accepted behaviour pattern. The statistics published by the Registrar General show that out of all maternities in England and Wales during the period 1951-1955 over 12 per cent were conceived extramaritally. Of these slightly over half were legitimated by marriage before the birth of the child (Statistical Review, 1955). Of first legitimate maternities only, 20.5 per cent were conceived premaritally in 1956 (ibid., 1956). Illegitimacy is of course also connected with the unsuitability of contraceptive methods, a matter that has been discussed above. The alleged high incidence of cohabitation (which was not borne out in the Seaport survey) is linked with the very real difficulties that the legal processes of divorce presented to families of this type before 1949 when the Legal Aid system was established. Other 'abnormalities' mentioned by Blacker include alcoholism, cruelty to wife or children, venereal disease, epilepsy, psychosis or neurosis, other physical defects, and gambling. A good many of these indices have never been systematically assessed, and the evidence of the Seaport survey suggests that neither gambling nor alcoholism is widespread. As far as physical or mental defects are concerned they are of course a real handicap to the wage earner, and the sooner this is overcome administratively by additional sheltered work opportunities for the disabled, the easier it will be for the families at present afflicted by inadequate services of this kind. Certainly, none of these defects are confined to one social stratum of society. Furthermore, it is often not taken into consideration that physical or mental defect, or illness may be the main causative factor in the deterioration of a family's living conditions if social links are severed. This goes for drinking and gambling habits as well; the gambler of the stock exchange or the race course, however, can afford to indulge in this 'character defect' because he happens to have a larger margin of spendable income.

'Mis-spending' is also often mentioned as characteristic of these families. It is often forgotten that these families belong to the lowest income groups and they have a much larger number of children than the national average. Budgeting, therefore, has to be considerably more exact, and margins, if they exist at all, are much smaller than they would be in other income groups. The Seaport survey showed that the housewife is put to solve a task far beyond her capacity. It is assumed that she informs herself of daily price fluctuations, that she buys in the cheapest market only, and that she has the strength of character to refrain from an occasional temptation to buy the inessential. Any deviation from such a pattern is called 'mis-spending'. The fact that higher income groups have considerably larger margins and are not subject to public scrutiny does not preclude the existence of mis-spending among them. Among the families of the research set the outlay of a shilling on cream buns may mean that there is not enough money to pay the rent, which may be the beginning of a history of rent arrears, ultimately leading to eviction. Saying this does not imply that all debts are incurred because of occasional indulgence; in the Seaport research set there were quite a few mothers of very limited capabilities who found budgeting on a weekly basis too much to cope with. But the percentage of parents who spent heavily on quite inessential articles was small. It was rare for both parents to do it; in the families where it occurred it was either the father or the mother. The more usual pattern was that of the father who deprived the family of a portion of his wages. But since no sociological survey has been undertaken of gambling habits of other income groups it seems premature to single out these families under the heading of 'mis-spending'. Not only are they accused of an inability to make ends meet, but also account is too rarely taken of the fact that they are forced to buy in the most expensive way, by 'check' or 'club' payments, or some form of hire-purchase, since they never have enough money to pay cash for major items. Furthermore, clothes are often bought second-hand, or are of such cheap quality that they cannot last long. A second pair of shoes cannot be afforded in a large family, which makes repairs impossible. The Women's

Group on Public Welfare (1943) drew attention to the serious problems of buying under such conditions. In describing 'clubs' run by companies for the purpose of providing credit it is stated that the profit of such companies is mostly derived from the commission taken from the shopkeepers. One witness stated that the usual commission for clothing clubs was 17½ per cent from the shops where purchases are made; for each pound voucher issued the clothing club pays the shopkeeper 16s 6d. The shops that deal with clothing clubs then set a higher retail price in order to cover part of the commission allowed. Usually, a premium of 1s od in the pound is charged to the members if the check is taken in advance of the completion of payments. The repayments are collected by agents who again are paid on a commission basis. Hire-purchase payments cannot normally be made by people who have not enough cash for the down-payment, but sometimes club checks are taken as deposits. In addition to the interest payable on the hire-purchase agreement the customer has then to find the interest on the club check. Another frequent method of acquiring durable goods is to buy from the door-to-door salesmen, who work on a commission basis, selling not always the most essential goods at prices that are not always competitive.* In the home interviews I had with mothers purchases of family photographs, coloured and framed, ladies' winter boots, handbags, and so on were mentioned, and it appeared that the women were not always sure either of the price of the articles or of the duration of their weekly payments. All these ways of purchasing durable goods are extremely costly, and penalize the lowest income group most heavily. To hold these people entirely responsible for financial mismanagement shows ignorance of the economic position in which they find themselves.

The final and perhaps most vital point concerns attitudes to the social services. The accusations in this field are contradictory. Some observers allege that these families usually manage to get help from various sources simultaneously, whereas others say that it is typical of so-called 'problem families' that they don't make full use of the services at their disposal. The failure to

* An article in The Times of November 23, 1959, speaks of the 'Menace of "Doorstep Pests" in council estates. Weakwilled tenants are coaxed into too much credit buying'.

respond and to profit from advice, mentioned by Stephens (1945) and others, defiance of authority, and what sometimes appears to be an active desire to live in bad environmental conditions, point to the existence of feelings of anxiety and insecurity; and a general impression of immaturity is gained by observers in the psychiatric field. It is probably this trait which the community in general finds most difficult to accept. Welfare-state legislation is based on the assumption that the citizen will make full and intelligent use of the social services and will give in return what lies within his capacity. The deviant will be coerced into this pattern. There is no provision yet for curative services for those whose mental state does not allow coercion but who are not sufficiently ill to be given psychiatric treatment. The social services as they are at present administered are sometimes unacceptable because of their authoritative appearance and their power to apply official sanctions. What appears to be a state of immaturity among some of the parents referred to co-ordination committees may be little more than a regressive response to continuous frustration situations, a point I discussed more fully elsewhere (Wilson, 1959). In such a state of mind it becomes very difficult to accept and act upon the advice of, say, a health visitor who is concerned about the state of the baby or the bedding; or to follow out the instructions of the housing visitor concerning redecorations which, if not carried out, will lead to eviction. Failure in the final analysis does not lie in the so-called immaturity of the group, but in the inadequacies of the social services which do not yet, as a rule, include skilled curative services. This point has been discussed in detail by Collis (1958). Beginnings have been made in the voluntary field with such organizations as the Family Service Units, and also in some local authorities where psychiatric social workers and other trained social workers are engaged to deal specifically with families who need therapeutic handling. But the number of those in the field is still too small to have an impact on the situation.

In summing up, it may be said that community attitudes towards this deviant group are at present heavily loaded with fear, which expresses itself in many negative and aggressive ways. It is to be hoped that just as in the field of mental illness the initial attitude of hostility, which resulted in punishment of the mentally deranged was turned into a constructive attitude which recognized the need for treatment, so in the field of social deviation community attitudes will change. As knowledge increases about the extremely heterogeneous group of people who at present are lumped together under the label of 'problem families', we will begin to see their many problems no longer as a threat to our living standards but as a challenge to us as social reformers.

What are the sociological implications of this? What sort of society is able to carry families of this type? Again and again industrialized society throws up 'problem families'—families which cannot adapt themselves to a pattern of life in which personal initiative, intelligent action, decision-making ability, and the formation of purpose are at a premium. Modern life in its extreme form is urbanized, individualized; the close-knit community life of the village becomes more and more a-typical. In the urban setting the family has to rely primarily on internalized values. What is right and what is wrong in constantly changing situations is supposed to be understood by the modern adult city dweller, and guidance and advice are looked for in reference groups which are not linked with the neighbourhood group. Systems of ideas are transmitted by means of communication across and above the neighbourhood unit; the mind of the city dweller is fed by newspapers, the radio, television, the theatre, books, films, discussion groups and all the rest. Modern man, if he is to stand the pace of city life, must be intelligent, quick, sensitive, able, and conversant with the multitude of roles which he is expected to play. He can afford to be highly mobile, as he relies little, if at all, on the neighbourhood as a comforter in crises; his friendships are formed irrespective of geographic location. But there is another type of city dweller— a type described in recent community studies—the working-class city dweller who lives in a close-knit community of friends and relations, who conforms to local patterns of behaviour and who derives comfort and support in times of crisis from his own relations or near neighbours who have been known to him for many years. The carrying quality of the neighbourhood, the close-knit relationship system of working-class areas as described by Young and Willmott (1957), is much the same as the quality of village life; Bethnal Green is the village within the metropolis whose internal working mechanism is not much different from that described by Frankenberg (1957) in a village on the Welsh border. When Frankenberg relates the story told by a village inhabitant: 'If you punch my wife on the nose, the whole village will come running', he implies that morality is safeguarded by a community of people who feel they belong together and have social responsibilities towards one another. Morality, Firth (1951) says, has important social functions and exists in virtue of them; in fact, the existence of a social system necessitates a moral system for its support. In the village the moral system is passed on from generation to generation primarily by custom; the highly educated city dweller supplants the customary system by one which he is continuously recreating out of internalized experiences. In an interesting study of twenty families in London, Bott (1957) shows the differences in norm formation between the close-knit community on one hand and the typical city-dweller on the other. She says that members of close-knit communities are likely to develop a high degree of consensus on norms and ideology because of their frequent interaction with one another. Errors of judgment are rapidly corrected, and the community is almost inevitably used as a reference group. On the other end of the scale the family who has broken away from the close-knit group internalizes standards in accordance with individual needs and adjusts these as experience demands. Bott does not discuss the function of intelligence in the various social network systems, but it is obvious from the information she supplies concerning occupations that the families who have cut loose from the neighbourhood group and have developed their own individualized styles of living are more intelligent than those at the other end of the scale. The five families whose social contacts are not confined to the immediate neighbourhood and whose social network is loose-knit are two professionals, two semi-professionals and one clerical, whereas the only family living in a close-knit community is that of a semi-skilled manual worker living in a working-class district.

The families who formed the research set for the Seaport enquiry are not well endowed with intelligence. Most of the fathers are unskilled labourers and can be presumed to be of lower intelligence than even the semi-skilled manual worker described by Bott. It is indeed one of the difficulties of this group that they cannot acquire any skills owing to their low general capacities. The wives cannot be expected to develop an intelligent understanding of norms and ideology such as would be required from a family who has broken away from the supports of the neighbourhood community. As discussed in Chapter V, the research families are on the whole socially isolated; they are newcomers who have not been absorbed in the neighbourhood. Some of them had moved away from their original communities, others had been homeless for years and had ended up in squatters' camps or the Local Authority's Part Three Accommodation. Others again had been brought up in institutions and on setting up their families had moved from one set of furnished rooms to another until they were eventually provided with accommodation by the Local Authority. These people have not plunged into city life fully aware of its demands; they have not the qualities to make a go of it. Furthermore, they often have disabilities which prevent them from adopting a normal pattern of life, an additional handicap in the establishment of good relationships with new neighbours. In an old-established community such disabilities would be more easily tolerated. In his study of a Welsh village Frankenberg, for instance, describes the way in which the village coped with a woman suffering from paranoid delusions. She feared her belongings were going to be taken away and so she arranged to move everything to another house in the dark one night. Everybody in the village knew about this and co-operated in the game. What would happen to such a woman in a strange neighbourhood? Eccentric behaviour of a newcomer often creates fear and anger especially, when his living standards are considerably lower than those of his new neighbours. Newcomers are expected to conform to the patterns of the neighbourhood, and if they deviate they do not get the toleration and support which they might have had in their indigenous surroundings. Consequently they are socially isolated and cut off from the regulative relationships with neighbours. The mechanism by which behavioural rules are transmitted does not operate and the result is a non-willed deviation from social norms.

In that sense 'neglect-delinquency' as a social phenomenon should be seen, not as a manifestation of a specific sub-culture, but as an index of breakdown of a culture. Conglomerations of city dwellers with a high degree of mobility find themselves in an environment which will not extend its supportive relationship system to them, and yet they have not the individual strengths to create their own standards of morality. In the absence of cultural forces of interaction which shape life into a pattern of give-and-take, these socially isolated families are in danger of regressing to the animal level of survival with all the losses in terms of security and thwarting of individual development that this entails.

CHAPTER X

SOME PRACTICAL PROPOSALS

THE young delinquents described on these pages are not easily cured by the various methods of treatment that the courts have at their disposal. They are more likely to be recidivists than their playmates who come from better homes. The numbers involved in the Seaport enquiry were small; just under 100 boys and a similar number of girls were found to be of an age at which they could be brought before a juvenile court. Four-fifths of the boys and one-third of the girls will have appeared before court and found guilty of an indictable offence by the time they are seventeen years old. There are another 160 younger children at present growing up in the same families who will reach the courts within the next decade or so. What immediate preventive action could be undertaken to alleviate the situation?

In searching for new ways of action two points ought to be kept in mind. The first one has been emphasized throughout the preceding pages: the families who served as case material for the investigation are a heterogeneous group of people whose only common denominator has been their inability to cope with the various demands put upon them by society. Some of these families, as has been pointed out, have weathered the critical child-bearing years of the mother and are now on the way to adopting a more normal living pattern. Others show no signs of change, and the fundamental difficulty may be a permanent disability of the mother. There are other families in which the father is the unstable personality through whom living patterns are disturbed. In others again, living conditions have deteriorated because the father through some disability has been unable to remain in work, or when in work has not earned enough to support a large family. Whatever the family constellation, delinquency appeared as a by-product of a low standard of living coupled with child neglect. In searching for the right type of remedial action it must be remembered that no overall solution can be found which would be appropriate for all families, different as they are from one another in their essential characteristics. A number of practical suggestions, however, might not be out of place concerning the alleviation of immediate obstacles which are primarily of a material nature. In a good many cases this may be all that is needed. In other cases, however, certain personality problems would necessitate the help of specialized psychiatric services. The second point has also been elaborated previously, and it concerns the nature of the problem. The delinquency arising out of the way of living that has been described on these pages is a family problem, not an individual child-problem. Prevention must therefore lie in the treatment of the family situation, and not entirely in the treatment of the child.

It has been demonstrated, in the first place, that there are certain patterns of adverse economic conditions in all the families which are at least partly responsible for the existence of physical neglect of the children. The tables correlating the fathers' work and health records with the mothers' health records and the sizes of the families have shown that the struggle to bring up very large families on low incomes is a test that would break all but the most resourceful and capable personalities. It seems imperative that the anomalous position of the low-income earner who brings up a family of six or more children on a total income that is below subsistence level should be tackled at once. There is a strong case for raising family allowances progressively so that each additional child receives a slightly larger sum. There should, in addition, be increments for older children similar to those paid by the National Assistance Board. By raising family allowances the man with a low income and large family would no longer be induced to leave work voluntarily, as he would financially be better off while in work.

Secondly, consideration should be given to those families who for one reason or another are permanently dependent on state-maintained incomes. It has been shown by Shaw and Bowerbank that there is not sufficient margin for expenses on clothing and household replacements even for those who are in receipt of full allowances; it is even more difficult for those whose allowances have been cut to match them to former spending money. There is an urgent need to amend Assistance Board regulations so as to enable long-term clients to claim regular lump-sum payments for the acquisition of clothing and household requirements.

Thirdly, it has been shown that the size of the family is a burden that none of the mothers are able to carry. Family planning clinics have been found to be of little service. There is an urgent need for methods more suitable under conditions such as have been described above.

Fourthly, there is a great need for the establishment of nursery schools for children between two and five years old. Such nurseries should be available in the first place for mothers of large young families; and an essential service connected with them should be free transport to relieve the mothers of the duty of taking and fetching their children. These nurseries, even if open only during the morning, would help considerably in lightening the burden of the mothers who have no other assistance at home. They would also give an opportunity for the small child to be introduced to a regulated and disciplined environment. This might reduce the difficulties that the five-year-old has at present on entering the infant school. (For details of an experimental nursery school of this type see Appendix XIV.)

Fifthly, and this is perhaps the most vital point, it appears that one of the main difficulties in the lives of these families is the rejection of the family by their kin; or else the absence of kin for other reasons. They have to rely on their own resources in solving their sometimes unsolvable problems. The need for specialized help in the form of a trusted family advisor is imperative. Enough has been written in other places about the type of service needed, and the success of the approach evolved by the Family Service Units is proof of the need for such a service. The Report of the Ingleby Committee on Children and Young Persons (1960), one of whose terms of reference was the consideration of methods to prevent the suffering of children through neglect in their own homes, stresses the importance of intensive family casework which the Family Service Units provide: 'The Units are probably the best known of the organizations which tackle the "problem" family, and we were greatly impressed by the accounts we received from all quarters of the work they carry out'. Looking into the future, the Report recommends a reorganization of the various services concerned with the family so that a unified 'family service' is available to those who need it. The provision of such a service should be a duty of the local authority, who should have powers to do casework in the family to prevent the neglect of children in their own homes.

If such preventive measures were undertaken on the family level, a good deal of wastage at present occurring in the field of the social services could be cut out. The co-ordination committees which now often find themselves unable to carry out such preventive work for lack of social workers, would be immeasurably strengthened in their concerted efforts. Their discussions frequently have to remain on the diagnostic level. The complex problem of housing so-called unsatisfactory tenants can only be touched on here. A trusted social worker who helps the parents budget is of invaluable assistance to a local authority's housing department. The reception of children into care of the local authority for housing reasons only is an abuse of our rights to remove children for their own benefit. Prosecution for neglect and the removal of children may still be the best solution when there is no constructive policy; it may in some cases be better from the children's point of view to be removed. But a saner policy is that which deals with the removal of difficulties on the family level, so as to enable the children to live a normal family life. The wastage of human material and of economic resources in dealing with the problem of juvenile delinquency arising out of such conditions is out of proportion to the relatively small number of families that are involved in creating the problem. Two children in an approved school cost the nation more than the salary of an experienced social worker, who by carrying a case load of a dozen families with six children each would help to keep many more children out of a delinquent career. Family casework on a preventive level has, so far, not been advocated as a method of delinquency therapy, and the solutions commonly advocated, such as reform homes for mothers, probation of mothers or children, and approved schools, do not tackle the problem at its roots. The need for treatment exists long before the child appears in court.

It may be argued that some of the families who have been described on these pages can never be expected to profit from any guidance that they might receive from the social worker. This is very probably true in cases as, for instance, that of a family in which both parents are borderline mental defectives. In such a case all that can be aimed at would be a policy of containment during the critical child-bearing and child-rearing years of the mother. She would very likely need more time than, but probably not so much specialized help as, a mentally unstable mother. The aim must be one of support during the critical period, to be withdrawn gradually if and when the family is sufficiently strengthened to carry on without it. Such support is possible only on an emotional basis of trust and confidence.

In conclusion, let us remember that none of the conditions described above are offered as complete explanations of the families' failures to cope with life. All they may do is to point out weaknesses in the social fabric that need further study in the search for a solution to the problems of these families. While ultimately it is the personality of the parents that makes or mars family life, the conditions in which they have to work may be such that even those with reasonable resources may succumb in continuous frustration situations. It is here that the challenge lies to the social reformer and to the social worker: whereas the reformer of a former generation promised Heaven on earth, the promise now must be limited to the clearing away of obstacles and the offer of support to those who lack the strength to cope alone with crises.

APPENDICES

I. Agencies consulted 166

II. Interview sheet for social workers 167

III. Illnesses of fathers 169

IV. Illnesses of mothers 171

V. Rate of entry into delinquency 172

VI. Cumulative delinquent rate 173

VII. Delinquency rate as a function of age 174

VIII. Delinquency of research set and control group 175

IX. Age, sex and offences of boys and girls 176

X. Parental relations 178

XI. Parental convictions 181

XII. Types of offences of parents 182

XIII. Parental convictions and juvenile convictions 185

XIV. An experimental nursery school 186

AGENCIES CONSULTED

THE writer is greatly indebted to the following agencies for the patient provision of much help and information.

Child Guidance Clinic
Children's Department
Criminal Records Department
Education Department
Employment Exchange
Housing Department
Magistrates' Clerks' Office
National Assistance Board
National Society for the Prevention of Cruelty to
    Children
Probation Office
Public Health Department
Seaport Mental Hospital
Youth Employment Bureau.

APPENDIX II

INTERVIEW SHEET FOR SOCIAL WORKERS AND HEALTH VISITORS

THE interview consisted of two parts. The first, Part I below, contained definite questions, asked of each social worker or health visitor, to which definite answers were expected. The second, Part II below, consisted of a number of headings by which a general conversation was guided. Very often the most interesting and useful information about the family emerged during the second part of the interview.

The actual interview sheet contained three parallel columns, so that the answers of up to three social workers or health visitors could be recorded side by side for easy comparison. Only one column is reproduced here, so that the questions can be set out with greater clarity.

Standardized replies were provided for questions ii, iii, ix and xii, so that assessments by different workers could be compared easily.

Name of social worker   Code number
or health visitor: of family:
Frequency of visits?

Part I

 (i) Composition of family?
 (ii) Assessment of neighbourhood: Good
             Fair
             Poor
             Very poor
 (iii) Condition of home: Good
         Fair
         Poor
         Very Poor
 (iv) Overcrowded for sleeping?
 (v) Health of father?
 (vi) Intelligence of father?
 (vii) Health of mother?
 (viii) Intelligence of mother?
 (ix) Marital relationship: Normal
          Friction
          Indifference

(x) Separation or desertion at any time?
(xi) Habits leading to disturbance of home life?
(xii) Cohesion of family: Cohesive
                              Some elements of cohesion
                              Unintegrated
(xiii) Discipline exercised by father?
(xiv) Supervision exercised by mother?
(xv) Affection shown by father for children?
(xvi) Affection shown by mother for children?

Part II
(xvii) Family planning
(xviii) Income
(xix) Rent
(xx) Debts
(xxi) Clothing clubs
(xxii) Insurance
(xxiii) Pawnbroker
(xxiv) Money lender
(xxv) Betting
(xxvi) Other problems.

APPENDIX III

ILLNESSES OF FATHERS

1. Fathers on register of disabled persons (ten in all).

Case
5 Deafness; disability pension
6 One kidney removed; disability pension
12 Asthma
21 Deformed hip from accident at age 14
25 Heart disease, burst right ear drum, very poor eyesight
34 Heart disease, eye injury while at work, disability pension
39 Heart disease
41 Bronchial trouble, deafness; in receipt of pension (not known whether related to above troubles)
45 Accident to right hand
46 Tuberculosis

2. Ill-health not registered as a disablement (twelve in all).
7 Rupture, wears belt
8 Heart disease (has died of thrombosis after closing date of this investigation)
20 Duodenal ulcers, several attacks of pneumonia
22 Nephritis
23 Duodenal ulcers
27 Chronic chest trouble
29 Gastric ulcers
30 Bronchial catarrh, prematurely senile
33 Gastric ulcers
35 Gastric ulcers, high blood pressure
38 Pernicious anaemia
42 Bronchrectasis

3. Mental illnesses (seven in all).
(Diagnoses supplied by medical practitioners or psychiatrists, except for case 10, who has had no treatment).
10 Twice charged with attempted suicide. (Police record of interference with passengers on public transport, wounding and assaulting police)
13 Psychopathic personality, mentally unstable, feebleminded, socially and morally degenerate
18 Psychopathic personality, with neurotic symptoms

24 Psychoneurosis, gastric trouble
40 Paranoid schizophrenia with hallucinations and ideas of reference and some delusions
44 Psychopath
47 Psychopathic personality, with poor level of intelligence

The total number of fathers with some type of disability or ill-health is thus 29.

ILLNESSES OF MOTHERS

1. Ill-health (12 cases in all).

Case
5 Asthma, concussion when aged 16 and consequent operation at back of head, nervous debility, occasional blackouts
7 Anaemia, undernourishment
10 Kidney trouble, one kidney removed
11 Diabetes, periodic blackouts
14 Anaemia, undernourishment
19 Anaemia, undernourishment
28 Chest trouble and obesity
31 Hernia, wears belt
40 Chronic chest trouble
41 Heart trouble, varicose veins
46 Phlebitis, gynaecological operation
47 Collapsed lung, patient at chest clinic, anaemia

2. Mental illnesses (four cases in all).
4 Depression following attempted suicide
18 Psychoneurosis, periodic depressions, asthma
43 Psychopathic personality, hysteria, periodic superficial depression
52 Psychopathic personality, mentally dull
(Diagnoses supplied by psychiatrists)

The total number of mothers with some type of diagnosed disability or ill-health is thus 16.

APPENDIX V

RATE of entry into delinquency, being the percentage of boys and girls so far non-delinquent who become delinquent during year of age stated.

Year of age	Research-family boys	Control-group boys	Research-family girls	Control-group girls
8	9%	2%	0%	0%
9	6	4	3	0
10	15	4	6	0
11	17	10	4	1*
12	25	6	5	1½
13	32	10	15	0
14	(14)	(4)	(3)	(5½)
15	(20)	(0)	(10)	(9)
16	(17)	..	(4)	..

*The figures for control-group girls all arise from a single shoplifting escapade in which four girls took part.

APPENDIX VI

CUMULATIVE delinquent rate as a function of age, being the number of boys or girls per hundred who have been delinquent at some time before or during the year of age stated.

Year of age	Research-family boys	Control-group boys	Research-family girls	Control-group girls
8	9%	2%	0%	0%
9	14	6	3	0
10	24	9	9	0
11	33	18	8	1
12	48	24	13	1½
13	63	24	28	0
14	68	37	28	5½
15	68	33	32	4
16	72	..	31	..
17	85	..	28	..
18	82	..	27	..

Note. The figures are calculated independently at each age for the children actually in the picture at that age. Removal of children to approved schools etc. reduces the cumulative rates at the higher ages. The true cumulative rates, if they could be ascertained, would be somewhat higher. All figures in the control-group girls column arise from a single incident of shoplifting.

APPENDIX VII

DELINQUENCY rate as a function of age, being the number of convictions per hundred boys or girls during the year of age stated.

Year of age	Research-family boys	Control-group boys	Research-family girls	Control-group girls
8	10%	2%	0%	0%
9	14	7	4	0
10	24	4	6	0
11	22	18	4	1*
12	37	8	10	1½
13	52	13	20	0
14	35	12	13	5½
15	32	(6)	20	0
16	(28)	(0)	11	0
17	(69)	..	(3)	..

Each conviction is counted only once, even though there may be several charges and other offences taken into consideration. *All figures in the column for control-group girls arise from a single shoplifting episode.

APPENDIX VIII

DELINQUENCY IN RESEARCH FAMILIES AND IN CONTROL GROUPS

THIS table gives the total numbers (T) passing through each age, the numbers delinquent (D) at that age, and the number of convictions (C) at that age.

| | Research families | | Control groups Docks | | Broomhill | |
| | Boys | Girls | Boys | Girls | Boys | Girls |
Age	T D C	T D C	T D C	T D C	T D C	T D C
8	97 9 10	97 — —	62 2 2	70 — —	63 1 1	52 — —
9	84 8 12	91 3 4	62 6 6	70 — —	63 2 3	52 — —
10	74 14 18	80 5 5	60 1 1	70 — —	54 4 4	41 — —
11	60 12 13	71 3 3	52 8 10	55 1 1	47 4 8	30 — —
12	52 17 19	63 6 6	48 1 1	44 1 1	31 5 5	24 — —
13	46 17 24	54 8 11	37 4 4	32 — —	24 5 5	16 — —
14	37 13 13	47 6 6	25 2 3	28 2 2	9 1 1	8 — —
15	25 7 8	41 5 8	15 — —	18 — —	3 1 1	5 — —
16	18 5 5	35 4 4	8 — —	7 — —	— — —	— — —
17	13 7 9	29 1 1	— — —	— — —	— — —	— — —
18	11 4 5	26 3 4	— — —	— — —	— — —	— — —

AGE, SEX AND OFFENCES OF DELINQUENT RESEARCH-FAMILY CHILDREN

(i) Indictable offences

Offence	8 M	8 F	9 M	9 F	10 M	10 F	11 M	11 F	12 M	12 F	13 M	13 F	14 M	14 F	15 M	15 F	16 M	16 F	17 M	17 F	Total M	Total F
Larceny																					97	32
from meter	-	-	-	-	1	-	-	-	-	-	1	-	-	-	-	-	-	-	-	-		
from person	-	-	-	-	1	-	-	-	1	-	1	1	-	-	-	-	-	-	-	-		
in dwelling	2	-	3	1	2	-	3	2	3	1	1	-	6	2	6	-	8	-	-	-	34	6
by finding	-	-	-	-	-	-	-	-	-	1	-	-	-	-	-	-	-	-	-	-		
shoplifting	1	-	-	-	1	1	-	-	2	-	1	3	2	-	-	5	-	-	-	-	7	9
of bicycle	1	-	1	1	-	-	1	-	-	-	-	-	-	-	-	-	-	-	-	-		
unspecified	6	-	3	-	4	1	7	-	8	-	9	11	6	2	2	2	2	-	1	1	48	17
Breaking																					41	8
shop, store, office	1	-	1	1	1	-	2	1	4	1	1	-	5	1	5	-	6	-	-	-		
factory	-	-	1	-	1	-	-	-	-	-	-	-	-	-	1	-	-	-	-	-		
house, school	1	-	-	-	3	-	1	1	-	-	1	1	5	2	-	-	1	-	-	-		
attempt	-	-	-	-	-	-	-	-	-	-	1	-	-	-	-	-	-	-	-	-		
Malicious or wilful damage	1	-	2	-	1	-	3	-	1	-	7	-	2	-	2	-	3	-	2	-	24	—
Receiving	-	-	-	-	-	-	-	-	-	-	1	-	-	-	-	-	-	-	1	-	2	—
Robbery	-	-	-	-	-	-	1	-	-	-	-	-	-	-	-	-	1	-	-	-	2	—
Assault with intent to rob	-	-	1	-	-	-	-	-	-	-	-	-	-	-	-	-	-	-	-	-	1	—
Assault	-	-	-	-	-	-	-	-	-	-	-	-	-	-	-	-	-	1	-	1	—	2
Burglary	-	-	-	-	-	-	-	-	-	-	-	-	-	-	-	-	-	-	1	-	1	—

(ii) Non-indictable offences

Offence	\<br\> 8 \<br\> M F	\<br\> 9 \<br\> M F	Age and sex of offender\<br\> 10 \<br\> M F	\<br\> 11 \<br\> M F	\<br\> 12 \<br\> M F	\<br\> 13 \<br\> M F	\<br\> 14 \<br\> M F	\<br\> 15 \<br\> M F	\<br\> 16 \<br\> M F	\<br\> 17 \<br\> M F	Total\<br\>\<br\> M F
Truancy etc.	3 -	1 1	3 4	5 1	2 2	3 3	3 2	- 2	1 -	- -	21 15
Larceny of growing fruit	- -	- -	1 -	- 1	- 1	1 -	1 -	1 -	- -	- -	3 2
In need of care and protection arising out of delinquency	2 -	- -	- -	- -	- -	- -	- -	- -	- -	- -	2 —
Beyond control	- -	- -	1 -	- -	- -	- -	- -	- -	- -	- -	1 —
Taking and driving away	- -	- -	- -	- -	- -	- -	- -	- -	- -	1 -	1 —
Obscene language	- -	- -	- -	- -	- -	- -	- -	- -	- 1	- -	— 1

APPENDIX X

PARENTAL RELATIONS

THE following summaries are based on the answers to questions ix, x, xi and xii (page 167) addressed to social workers and health visitors, on the records of the matrimonial court, and sometimes on evidence from other sources. To avoid the possibility of individual families being identified the code numbers are omitted. The abbreviations SW (social worker), HV (health visitor), N (normal), F (friction), I (indifference), C (cohesive), E (some elements of cohesion), and U (unintegrated) are used.

Marital relationship HV	SW	Matrimonial court	Separation	Illegitimate children	Family cohesion HV	SW
I-F	F	no	Mother left for 6 weeks	no	U	E
F	—	no	no	no	U-E	—
Mother dead		—	—	no	C	C
I	F	—	no, but see note i	2 of father	C	E
F	—	Sep. orders '50, '52, '55	Father left	2 of mother	C-E	—
F	—	no	no	no	?	—
N	F	no	Father left (returned)	1 of mother	C	—
F	—	Sep. order '52.	Father left (returned)	no	E	—
N	—	no	Separated for same time	2 of mother	C	—
F	N	no	no see note ii	no	C	C
N	—	no	no see note iii	one of mother?	C	—
N	—	no	no	no	E-U	—
N	—	no	no Incest?	no	C	—
F	—	Sep. orders '53, '55	Father left (returned)	2 of mother	Don't know	
N	—	no	no	no	C	—
N	I	no	no	no	C	E
F	F	no	no	no	E	E
N	F	no	no	no	C	C
N	(F)	no	no	no	C	(U)
F	—	no	no	no	E	—
I	(I)	no	no, but see note iv	no	U	(U)

Marital relationship		Matrimonial court	Separation	Illegitimate children	Family cohesion	
HV	SW				HV	SW
N	(?)	no	no, see note v	no	C	(E)
N	(N)	no	no	no?	C	(C)
N	F	no	no, but see note vi	1 of mother	C	C
—	—	no	note vii	—	—	—
F	(?)	Sep. orders '50	note viii	4 of father	U	(U)
N	(F)	no	no	no	C	(C)
N	(F)	no	no, but see note ix	no	C	?
N	(N)	no	see note x	no	C	C
N	N	no	no	no	C	C
N	N	no	no	no	C	C
I	F	no	no?	no	E	— note xi
F	—	no	no	no	U	— note xii
F	F	no	note viii	no	C	U
N	F	no	no note v	no	E	E
N	—	no	no note xiii	no	E	—
Mother divorced		Sep. order '55	Father deserted	no	U	—
N	N	no	note xiv	no	C	C
?	—	no	?	no	E	—
—	—	Sep. order '55	Father now left	no	—	—
Father dead		no	note xv	2 of mother	U	—
F	—	Sep. order '55	Father left several times	no	C	—
F	—	Sep. order '45	Father left, Mother left, both back	no	E	—
N	—	no	no?	no	C	—
N	—	no	note xvi	no	C	—
N	N	no	note xvii	no	C	C
N-F	—	no	no	no	E	—
—	—	?	?	no	—	—
N	—	no	no	no	C	—
—	—	no	note xviii	2 of mother	—	—
N	—	no	no	1 of mother	?	—
F	—	Sep. order '50	note xix	1 of mother?	E	—

Notes to Appendix X

   i Father cohabits, and has been convicted of indecent assault.
  ii Second marriage of father.
 iii Second marriage of mother.
 iv Father visits neighbour (single woman).
   v Mother divorced.
 vi Mother associates with another man, and practises as prostitute.
 vii Mother has associated with four other men.
viii Father associates with other women.
  ix 'Uncle' lives with mother while father is in prison.
   x Father went to mother's mother with children, but returned.
 xi Father's first wife died.
 xii Two previous wives died.
xiii Mother widowed.
xiv Father left former wife for present mother.
 xv Mother associates with other men.
xvi Father deserted for a short period.
xvii Mother left first husband for present father.
xviii Mother cohabiting; six previous children in care.
 xix Father continually deserts.

APPENDIX XI

PARENTAL convictions for indictable and certain non-indictable offences. (A full list is given in appendix XII).

Neither parent convicted	20
Both parents convicted for child neglect only	2
One parent only convicted for child neglect	3
Father only convicted for an offence other than neglect	20
Mother only convicted for an offence other than neglect	5
Both parents convicted for offences other than neglect	2
Total	52

APPENDIX XII

CONVICTIONS OF PARENTS

Non-indictable offences of parents convicted of indictable offences are included, but parents convicted of non-indictable offences are not.

Offence	Family	Number of convictions Father	Mother
Larceny	1	8	—
	2	1	—
	3	1	—
	4	1	—
	5	2	—
	6	1	—
	7	—	3
	8	2	—
	9	1	—
	10	1	—
	11	5	—
	12	13	—
	13	5	—
	14	2	—
	15	2	2
	16	1	1
	17	—	1
	18	8	—
	19	3	—
	20	1	—
	21	10	—
	22	1	—
	23	7	—
	24	13	—
Breaking and entering	1	10	—
	12	5	—
	13	7	—
	18	3	—
	19	1	—
	21	1	—
	23	4	—
	24	4	—
Burglary	21	1	—

For reasons of non-identification the families have code numbers which are not identical with those in the text.

Father 21 had 66 cases of housebreaking and larceny taken into account, as well as the 11 convictions recorded above.

Offence	Family	Number of convictions	
		Father	Mother
False pretences	2	2	—
	7	—	5
	8	—	1
	25	—	1
	13	3	—
	15	2	5
	18	1	—
	26	2	—
Receiving	12	2	—
Malicious or unlawful wounding	4	1	—
	12	1	—
	27	—	1
	23	2	—
Wilful damage	2	2	—
	27	—	3
	23	2	—
Assault	2	1	—
	4	2	—
	6	1	—
	6	1	—
	12	1	—
	28	—	1
	17	1	—
	27	—	9
	18	2	—
	19	2	—
	23	10	—
	24	1	—
	29	4	—
Drunk and disorderly	2	1	—
	23	1	—
	24	2	—
Disorderly conduct	27	—	1
Indecent assault	5	4	—
	24	1	—
Indecent language	5	1	—
	18	1	—
	23	2	—
Aiding and abetting indecent prostitution	11	1	—
Indecent prints	5	1	—
Gaming	1	1	—
	5	4	—
	11	1	—
	20	2	—
	24	1	—

DELINQUENCY AND CHILD NEGLECT

Offence	Family	Number of convictions Father	Mother
Looting	23	1	—
Street betting	35	3	—
	20	2	—
Street hawking	23	2	—
Obscenity	23	1	—
	24	1	—
Ill-treatment of animal	14	1	—
	36	1	—
Attempted suicide	4	2	—
Neglect of family	8	1	—
Cruelty or neglect of children	30	—	1
	31	1	—
	9	4	1
	32	1	1
	11	1	1
	16	—	1
	17	2	2
	33	1	1
	21	1	—
	22	2	2
	34	—	1

APPENDIX XIII

CORRELATION of parental convictions and juvenile delinquencies. Convictions for child neglect not included.

	Age	Total number	Number delinquent	%
BOYS				
Parents not	8–13	19	9	47 }67
convicted	14–17	14	13	93
	18 up	5	5	100
Parent(s)	8–13	32	12	38 }42
convicted	14–17	11	6	55
	18 up	7	6	86
GIRLS				
Parents not	8–13	20	6	30 }34
convicted	14–17	12	5	42
	18 up	8	2	25
Parent(s)	8–13	24	2	8 }20
convicted	14–17	6	4	67
	18 up	10	6	60

APPENDIX XIV

AN EXPERIMENTAL
NURSERY SCHOOL IN SEAPORT

IN April 1960 a small nursery school for three to five year old children was set up by the Society of Friends in an endeavour to help mothers with large families and low incomes. The minimum number of children in the family to qualify for admission is five. Cases are referred by the Social Worker of the Public Health Department, by health visitors, by teachers, and by the Co-ordination Committee of the City Council. A generous offer of a voluntary youth club provided accommodation on one of the housing estates which contains a large group of sub-standard houses. It is here that one finds many families whose fathers have been out of work for long periods, mainly owing to physical or mental disabilities. There are many other families with hard-working fathers who, however, owing to their limited capabilities and the large sizes of their families have an income per head which is well below subsistence level. The mothers are frequently run down by childbirth, continuous money worries, bad diet, and no hope of help or an occasional holiday. There are 24 places in the nursery school, and the fifteen families whose children attend at the time of writing have 101 children between them.

Two trained nursery nurses are in attendance at the nursery school. In addition, local members of the Society of Friends come in and give a hand in a voluntary capacity. A service which was felt to be essential was the provision of transport for the children. The children are too small to get to the nursery school by themselves, in some cases there is a considerable distance from home to the school, and their clothing, especially footwear is pitifully inadequate. A local mini-bus proprietor collects the children from their homes at 9 a.m. and takes them home again at 12 noon. On many mornings the nursery nurses have to knock a mother up and help to dress the child to go to the nursery school. A meal of milk, bread and margarine, supplemented in the winter months by orange juice and cod liver oil, is given to the children on arrival.

The clothing of the children is frequently inadequate, especially during the cold and wet season. Often a child would arrive without a woolly, or without underwear. Shoes are usually plastic sandals or plimsolls or sometimes Wellingtons, often very worn out. Clothing

and footwear for the children and also for their families are continuously collected and re-distributed.

Many local well-wishers have helped in providing equipment.
Of all the efforts made two deserve special mention. The local
grammar schools for girls made contributions of money during the
first three terms of the nursery school to help children 'less fortunate
than themselves'. With the co-operation of the Governor and
Deputy Governor of the local prison a hobbies class for woodwork
was set up, in which the prisoners made a great number of toys
ranging from a toy shop and a rocking horse to a good selection
of Noah's animals.

The nursery school was started with eleven children and it was
gradually built up to the full complement of 24. The first few days
were difficult. The children were not used to having their activities
supervised, there was much fighting for toys and little idea about
what to do with a toy when one had managed to snatch it. There
was much wetting and one child soiled regularly. As time went on
the children became used to a certain routine, and this helped in
introducing newcomers to the nursery school. It is very rarely now
that there would be any fighting for a toy, because the children
know that each will have a turn with the most popular toys. The
children are learning surprisingly fast how to use scissors and other
small apparatus. Threading of beads and cutting out coloured paper
for patterns and drawing and painting are regular activities. There
is a general improvement of speech. Wetting, apart from the newcomer, has almost entirely disappeared. Breadcrusts are no longer
thrown on the floor. Politeness is encouraged, and a 'thank you'
for bread offered at their meal is beginning to be a regular response.
The children learn to wash before their meal, and help to clear
away and wash up their mugs.

A school nurse calls once a week for inspection and consultation.
The children often have verminous heads which are treated by the
nurses. Other infections such as impetigo are usually treated at
once to prevent spreading. A boy with a slight limp was taken to
hospital for x-ray examination, and a congenital deformity was
diagnosed. This child is now having remedial treatment. A girl with
a squint was fitted with glasses and will shortly have an operation.

Most of the mothers are very interested in the work of the nursery
school. It was on the suggestion of one of them that a collection
is made at the end of the week of any contribution that can be
spared to help defray expenses. The average sum per family voluntarily contributed is about one shilling. The mothers frequently

turn to the staff in moments of stress for advice and encouragement. Many enquiries are being made by other families for vacancies.

The public health department of the City Council is taking an active interest in the venture and is supporting it financially.

BIBLIOGRAPHY

ANDRY, R., *Delinquency and Parental Pathology*. London, 1960.

BAGOT, J. H., *Juvenile Delinquency*. Liverpool, 1941.

BENIANS, E. A., *Race and Nation in the United States*. Cambridge 1946.

BEVERIDGE, W., *Social Insurance and Allied Services*. HMSO, 1942.

BLACKER, C. P., (Editor), *Problem Families—Five Enquiries*. London, 1952.

BODMAN, F., *Case Conference*, 5, 99-104, 1958.

BOTT, E., *Family and Social Network*. London, 1957.

BOWERBANK, M., *Case Conference*, 4, 283-287, 1958.

BOWLBY, J., *Forty-four Juvenile Thieves, their characters and home life*. London, 1944.

BOWLBY, J., *Why Delinquency? The Case for Operational Research*. National Association for Mental Health, 1949.

BOWLBY, J., *et al. British Journal of Medical Psychology*, 29, 211-247, 1956.

BOWLBY, J., *Case Conference*, 4, 258, 1958.

British Medical Association and Magistrates Association Joint Committee. *Cruelty to and Neglect of Children*. London, 1956.

BURT, C., *The Young Delinquent*, London, 1925.

Central Housing Advisory Committee. *Unsatisfactory Tenants*, HMSO, 1955.

Children and Young Persons Act, 1933. HMSO.

Children and Young Persons (Amendment) Act, 1952. HMSO.

COHEN, A., *Delinquent Boys*. London, 1956.

COLLIS, A., *Social Work*, 15, 451-460, 1958.

Education (Miscellaneous Provisions) Act, 1953. HMSO.

FERGUSON, T., *The Young Delinquent in his Social Setting*. Oxford, 1952.

FIELD, D., and NEILL, D., *A Survey of New Housing Estates in Belfast*. Belfast, 1957.

FIRTH, R., *Elements of Social Organization*. London, 1951.

FLORENCE, C. S., *Progress Report on Birth Control*. London, 1956.

FORD, P., THOMAS, C. J., and ASHTON, E. T., *Problem Families. The Fourth Report of the Southampton Survey*. Oxford, 1955.

FRANKENBERG, R., *Village on the Border.* London, 1957.

FRIEDLANDER, K., *Psychoanalytic Approach to Juvenile Delinquency,* London, 1947.

GLASS, D. V., (Editor), *Social Mobility in Britain,* London, 1954.

GLUECK, S., and GLUECK, E., *Unravelling Juvenile Delinquency* Harvard, 1950.

GRÜNHUT, M., *Juvenile Offenders before the Courts.* Oxford, 1956.

HALL, M. P., *The Social Services of Modern England.* London, 1952.

HERSEY, R., In: *Readings in Industrial and Business Psychology,* edited by H. Karn *et al.* McGraw Hill, 1952.

HIMMELWEIT, H. T., HALSEY, A. H., and OPPENHEIM, A. N., *British Journal of Sociology,* 3, 148-172, 1952.

IRVINE, E., Research into Problem Families. *British Journal of Psychiatric Social Work,* 9, 24-33. 1954.

JEPHCOTT, A. P., and CARTER, M. P., *The Social Background of Delinquency.* University of Nottingham. (Restricted circulation), 1955.

Joint Circular from the Home Office, Ministry of Health and Ministry of Education. *Children Neglected or Ill-treated in their own Homes.* Appendix IX, Sixth Report of the Work of the Children's Department, 1951. HMSO.

JONES, H., *British Journal of Delinquency,* 8, 277-293, 1958.

JONES, H. E., Environmental Influences on Mental Development. In: *Manual of Child Psychology,* edited by L. Carmichael. New York, 1946.

JOSSELYN, I. M., *Psycho-Social Development of Children.* New York, 1948.

King George's Jubilee Trust. *Citizens of To-morrow,* 1955.

LEWIS, H., *Deprived Children,* Oxford, 1954.

MACIVER, R. M., *Society,* New York, 1937.

MACK, J. A., *British Journal of Delinquency,* 3, 302-304, 1953.

MANNHEIM, H., *Juvenile Delinquency in an English Middletown,* London, 1948.

MAYS, J. B., *Growing Up in the City,* Liverpool, 1954.

MERTON, R., *Social Theory and Social Structure,* New York, 1949.

Ministry of Labour *Gazette,* HMSO, 1961.

MOGEY, J. M., *Family and Neighbourhood,* Oxford, 1956.

BIBLIOGRAPHY

MORRIS, T. P., *The Criminal Area*, London, 1957.

National Assistance Act, 1948. HMSO.

National Assistance (Determination of Needs) Regulations, 1948, HMSO.

National Insurance Act, 1946, HMSO.

New Survey of London Life and Labour, vol. IX, 1935.

NISBET, J., *Eugenics Review*, 45, 31-40, 1953.

PHILP, A. F., and TIMMS, N., *The Problem of the Problem Family*, London, 1957.

RANKIN, T. G., *The Problem Family*. I.S.T.D. London, 1958.

RATCLIFFE, T. A., *The Problem Family*. I.S.T.D. London, 1958.

Registrar General's Statistical Review of England and Wales, 1955, Part III, pp. 19-20. 1956, Part II, p. 165. HMSO.

Report of the Committee on Children and Young Persons, 1960. HMSO.

ROWNTREE, B. S., and LAVERS, G. R., *Poverty and the Welfare State*, London, 1951.

SCHULZ, T., A 'human needs' Diet. *Oxford Bulletin of Statistics*, 18, 87-93, 1956.

Seventh Report on the Work of the Children's Department, 1955, HMSO.

SHAW, L., *Case Conference*, 4, 247-251, 1958.

SHAW, C. R., and MCKAY, H. D., *Juvenile Delinquency and Urban Areas*, Chicago, 1942.

SHERIDAN, M., The Intelligence of 100 Neglectful Mothers. *British Medical Journal*, 1, 91-93, 1956.

SPENCE, J., WALTON, W. S., MILLER, F. J. W., and COURTS, S. D. M., *A Thousand Families in Newcastle Upon Tyne*, Oxford, 1954.

SPENCER, J., *Eugenics Review*, 46, 29-38, 1954.

SPROTT, W. J. H., *The Listener*, June 9, pp. 1013-1014, 1955.

STEPHENS, T., *Problem Families*, Liverpool, 1945.

STEPHENSON, R. M., *British Journal of Sociology*, 9, 42-52, 1958.

TOWLE, C., *Common Human Needs*. American Association of Social Workers. New York, 1955.

TOWNSEND, P., Measuring Poverty. *British Journal of Sociology*, 5, 130-137, 1955.

VERNON, P. E., (Editor), *Secondary School Selection*. London, 1957.

WILSON, H. C., Problem Families and The Concept of Immaturity. *Case Conference*, 6, 115-118, 1959.

Women's Group on Public Welfare. *Our Towns—A Close-up.* Oxford, 1943.

Women's Group on Public Welfare. *The Neglected Child and His Family.* Oxford, 1948.

WOODWARD, M., *Low Intelligence and Delinquency.* I.S.T.D. London, 1955.

WOOTTON, B., *Social Science and Social Pathology*, London, Allen & Unwin, 1959.

YOUNG, M., and WILLMOTT, P., *Family and Kinship in East London.* London, 1957.

INDEX

Accident-proneness, 52-53
Adolescents, 77-80
Affectionless character, 125, 144
Alcoholism, 109, 152, 183
Andry, R., 128, 142, 145, 189
Anomie, 14, 16
Approved schools, 20, 79, 118, 163, 173
Area-delinquescence, 21, 25
Ashton, E. T., 34, 189

Bagot, J. H., 13, 189
Benians, E. A., 14, 189
Beveridge, W., 26, 53, 189
Black area, *see* High-delinquency area
Blacker, C. P., 152, 189
Bodman, F., 62, 189
Bott, E., 134, 157, 189
Bowerbank, M., 150, 161, 189
Bowlby, J., 125, 144, 189
British Medical Association, 30, 189
Burt, C., 13, 20, 189

Carlton Approved School, disturbances at, 20
Carmichael L., (Editor), 190
Carter, M. P., 21, 24, 25, 34, 190
Cases, *see* Families
Central Housing Advisory Committee, 93, 189
'Check' payments (clothing clubs), 153-154
Child Guidance Clinic, parental attitudes to, 102
Child-teacher relationships, 75, 139
Children and Young Persons Act 1933, 28
Amendment Act 1952, 28
Clothing clubs, 153-154
Cohen, A., 16, 17, 19, 189
Collis, A., 154, 189
Control group, 114, 117-122, 172-175
Co-ordination Committee, 29, 31, 34-38, 81, 163
Courts, S. D. M., 191; *see* Spence, J., *for citations in text*
Crime
and area studies, 19-20
and class, 13
and underprivileged areas, 13, 19, 21
ecological theory of, 14, 15
of parents, 141-144, 181-185
survey of literature, 13-22
Culture conflict, 14, 21

Debts, 32, 35, 38, 107-109
Delinquency
age of entry, 114-115, 121, 172
area studies, 21
cumulative rate, 118-120, 121
convictions per year of age, 119-120, 174, 175
definition, 112-113
national rate, 116-117
rate for city, 116-117, 121-122
rate of recidivism, 120
type of offences, 120, 121-122, 176-177
summary of findings, 122
Discretionary deductions, 56-57, 107
Divorce, 135-136, 152, 178-180
Door-to-door salesmen, 154

Education Act, 1944, 18
1870, 33
Miscellaneous Provisions, 1953, 71
Education, parental attitudes to, 105-107
Educational attainments, 68-69, 71-73
Educational prosecutions, 64, 71, 72
Emotional disturbances, 129-131
Employment
of adolescents, 77-80
of fathers, 49-58
of mothers, 58
Exceptional needs grants, 61

Families, 42, 43, 44, 178-184
no. 1, 47, 102, 141
2, 98, 106, 126
3, 48, 98, 101, 102, 103, 106, 127
4, 97, 106, 127, 132, 141, 171
5, 106, 169, 171
6, 101, 169
7, 101, 132, 169, 171
8, 140, 169
9, 140
10, 169, 171
11, 97, 171
12, 101, 169
13, 98, 132, 169
14, 101, 171
16, 106, 133, 140
17, 97, 99, 103
18, 169, 171
19, 105, 130, 140, 171
20, 98, 102, 127, 130, 133, 169
21, 102, 169
22, 127-128, 133, 140, 169

Families (*cont.*)
23, 101, 102, 133, 169
24, 98, 102, 105, 130, 133, 142, 170
25, 102, 169
26, 102, 131, 142
27, 101, 131, 140, 142, 169
28, 101, 133, 141, 171
29, 103, 169
30, 101, 169
31, 171
32, 131, 141
33, 101, 102, 128, 169
34, 101, 169
35, 169
37, 48, 99
38, 97, 133, 169
39, 169
40, 106, 170, 171
41, 98, 105, 128, 169, 171
42, 100, 127, 132, 169
43, 133, 171
44, 106, 132, 170
45, 97, 133, 169
46, 169, 171
47, 101, 128, 170, 171
48, 103, 106, 141
49, 133
50, 101, 105
51, 99, 106, 127, 132, 140
52, 171
Family allowances, 53-54, 161
Family planning, 26, 103-105, 150, 162
Family relationships, 124-141, 178-180
Family Service Units, 30, 37, 93, 155, 162-163
Ferguson, T., 14, 189
Field, D., 54, 189
Firth, R., 157, 189
Florence, C. S., 26, 104, 189
Ford, P., 34, 189
Frankenberg, R., 156, 158, 190
Friedlander, K., 24, 190

Gambling, 109, 152, 183, 184
Glass, D. V., 17, 190
Glueck, S., and E., 19, 125, 190
Grünhut, M., 20, 114, 116, 117, 122, 190

Hall, M. P., 26, 190
Halsey, A. H., 190; *see* Himmelweit, H. T., *for citation in text*
Hersey, R., 52, 190
High-delinquency area, 15, 21, 25, 117
Himmelweit, H. T., 18, 190
Hire purchase, 153
Human needs dietary, 58-60

Human needs level, *see* Subsistence level

Illegitimate children, 115, 130, 131
152, 178-179
Illness
of children, 65
of fathers, 40-44, 49, 169
of mothers, 44-46, 171
Ill-treatment of children, definition of, 30-31
of step-children, 89, 130-131
Immaturity, 62, 125, 154-155
Ingleby Committee, 162
Intelligence and social network 157-158
Intelligence quotient
of children, 64-73
of neglectful mothers, 151
and social class, 67
Intelligence tests, 65
Irvine, E., 62, 190

Jephcott, A. P., 21, 24, 25, 34, 190
Joint Circular from the Home Office, Ministry of Health and Ministry of Education, 1951, 29, 190
Jones, H., 15, 190
Jones, H. E., 67, 190
Josselyn, I. M., 139, 190

Karn, H., (Editor), 190
King George's Jubilee Trust, 79, 190
Kinship connectedness, 131-134, 156-159

Lavers, G. R., 191; *see* Rowntree, B. S., *for citation in text*
Legal aid, 152
Lewis, H., 129, 190
Lombroso, C., 13
Low-delinquency area, 21, 112, 122, 123

Mack, J. A., 20, 23, 190
Madge, C., 26, 104
Magistrates' Association, 30, 189
Maladjustment, 21, 72, 73, 85, 129-131
absence of, 73, 129
Maintenance orders, 135
Marital relationships, 134-138, 178-180
Mannheim, H., 13, 15, 190
Maternal deprivations, 144-145
Mays, J. B., 21, 25, 26, 190
McKay, H. D., 15, 191
Mental deficiency, 13, 26, 42, 43, 45, 46, 95, 115, 127, 151, 152

Mental illness, 13, 23, 26, 42, 43, 44, 169, 171
Mental retardation, 45, 125
Merton, R., 16, 17, 190
Miller, F. J. W., 191; *see* Spence, J., *for citation in text*
Middle class, 13, 17, 24
Mogey, J. M., 18, 190
Morris, T. P., 15, 191

National Assistance
  Act 1948, 27, 28
  allowances, 27, 47, 54, 55, 58, 60, 61, 85, 150, 161-162
National Council of Social Service, 29
National Health Service Act 1948, 32, 64, 100
National Insurance Act, 1946, 27
National Society for the Prevention of Cruelty to Children, 30, 37
Neglect of children, 30-31, 37, 89, 142, 143, 145, 146-147, 150, 151, 160, 181, 184
Neill, D., 54, 189
New Survey of London Life and Labour, 13, 191
Nisbet, J., 67, 191
Norm-formation, 157
Nursery schools, 162

Oppenheim, A. N., 190; *see* Himmelweit, H. T., *for citation in text*
Overcrowding, 82, 94

Parental crime, 141-144, 181-185
Parental handling of children, 124-131
Part-time work of wives, 58
Performance inadequacy, 25, 33, 35-39, 96-111, 148-155
Philp, A. F., 148, 191
Poverty, *see* Subsistence level
Poverty and crime, 13-14
Prediction studies, 19
Premarital sexual relations, 152
Preventive casework, 162-163
Probation, 20, 108
Problem families, 75-77, 148-156, 162
  sociological implications, 156-159
Prostitution, 79-80, 180
'Protestant virtues', 17

Rankin, T. G., 62, 191
Ratcliffe, T. A., 62, 191
Recidivism, 120

Rent arrears, 35, 82-86, 109
Rent rebate scheme, 36, 82-83
Rowntree, B. S., 60, 191

School attendance, 33, 36, 64, 68-73, 76-77, 105-107
Schulz, T., 59-60, 191
Separation orders, 134-136, 178-180
Seventh Report on the work of the Children's Department, 29-30
Shaw, C. R., 15, 191
Shaw, L., 61, 150, 161, 191
Sheridan, M., 151, 191
Social mobility, 16-19
Social services, 26-28, 151, 154-155, 163
Social workers, 93-94, 163, 167
Speech defects, 65, 74, 75
Spence, J., 26, 191
Spencer, J., 15, 191
Spending patterns, 107-109, 152-154
Sprott, W. J. H., 21, 191
Stephens, T., 104, 154, 191
Stephenson, R. M., 18, 191
Subsistence level, 26, 54, 56-58, 61, 124
Super-ego, 139-141

The Times, 56, 58, 154
Thomas, C. J., 34, 189
Timms, N., 148, 191
Toilet training, 74, 139
Towle, C., 63, 191
Townsend, P., 58, 60, 191
Truanting, 71, 112, 121, 122, 139, 177

Unsatisfactory tenants, 86, 90

Value judgments, 134, 156
Vernon, P. E., 68, 191

Walton, W. S., 191; *see* Spence, J., *for citation in text*
Welfare services, 26-27, 100-103, 110-111
Welfare State legislation, 26, 28
Whyte, William, 18
Willmott, P., 134, 149, 156, 192
Wilson, H. C., 155, 192
Women's Group on Public Welfare, 29, 30-31, 153, 192
Woodward, M., 67, 192
Wootton, B., 14, 54-55, 60, 192
Working class, 13-14, 17, 18, 134, 156

Young, M., 134, 149, 156, 192
Youth Employment Bureau, 78, 79

For Product Safety Concerns and Information please contact our EU
representative GPSR@taylorandfrancis.com
Taylor & Francis Verlag GmbH, Kaufingerstraße 24, 80331 München, Germany

www.ingramcontent.com/pod-product-compliance
Lightning Source LLC
Chambersburg PA
CBHW050445280326
41932CB00013BA/2254